TWO TRIBES

Rebuilding Team America in a Post-Truth World

Jim Hester

Motivational PRESS®
LEADERS IN GLOBAL PUBLISHING

Published by Motivational Press, Inc.
1777 Aurora Road
Melbourne, Florida, 32935
www.MotivationalPress.com

Manufactured in the United States of America.

ISBN: 978-1-62865-584-1

CONTENTS

PREFACE: MAKING A GAME PLAN **6**

PART ONE THE PRESEASON 11

1 DIVIDED **12**

2 TRUTH **40**

3 FAKE! **52**

4 FRIENDS **68**

5 DARKNESS **82**

PART TWO THE LONG SEASON. 94

DEFENSE. 95

6 HEALTH **96**

7 ENEMIES **108**

OFFENSE. 124

8 CLIMATE. **125**

9 WORK. **136**

SPECIAL TEAMS 144

10 RESPONSIBILITY (DEBT AND POVERTY) **145**

PART THREE A TEAM FOR THE AGES. 162

11 WILL IT BENEFIT ALL? (OR JUST ME?) **163**

12 IS IT TRUE? **175**

13 WOULD JESUS APPROVE? **187**

14 IS IT GOOD FOR OUR KIDS? **197**

15 WOULD LINCOLN CONCUR? **208**

16 CONCLUSION (POST-GAME COMMENTARY) **219**

FOOTNOTES **235**

ABOUT THE AUTHOR **249**

To Rachel, Riley, Anthony, and Becca, as well as the millions of other Americans who comprise the next generation. Remember that you're all on the same team. With truth, patriotism, and compassion as your guides, I am confident that you will work together to resolve problems through your collective and individual talents. With knowledge of the past, vision for the future, and with principled compromise, I am certain that you will improve, enhance, and rebuild this beautiful nation as it was meant to be, from two warring tribes to a team that is indivisible.

PREFACE

MAKING A GAME PLAN

In 2016, the Pew Research Center found that for the first time in its surveys, majorities in both political parties expressed *very* unfavorable views of the other party. It's not just that people disagree with the other party; sizable shares of both Democrats and Republicans say the other party causes them not just frustration but *fear* and *anger*. 70% of Democrats believe that Republicans are more close-minded than other Americans while nearly half of all Republicans believe that Democrats are immoral, lazy, and dishonest.[1] Almost half of all Americans believe that the positions of the other party are a *threat* to the nation's well-being. How are we going to solve problems if every other person you encounter is perceived as a threat?

Whatever your political leanings, we live in a complex world where ideological purity rarely solves problems that will only get worse. How can we face the many challenges that we are confronted with, some of which threaten our actual existence? There are no easy answers but we must find a way to become more united. We must stop looking at each other as the enemy. While we will probably never agree on certain "hot-button" issues, we should focus on certain universal issues that affect every man, woman, and child in America.

The Pledge of Allegiance provides the goal that we should strive for, which is "liberty and justice for all." Not just a few, not just the rich, powerful, or the lucky, but for all. While government cannot solve all problems, and cannot help all people equally, our leaders should focus on policies that will benefit the most people rather than the most powerful people.

Love him or hate him, Donald Trump is without doubt the most divisive president the United States has ever had. Since day one of his presidency, he has cast America in dark tones, describing it not as a city on a hill but full of "rusted-out factories scattered like tombstones" overwhelmed by "carnage" that only he can fix. However, we live in the greatest country ever created and its problems will be solved only by its leaders working together.

While tribalism and truth make up the big picture bookends of this book, its micro-lens is the first 18 months of the Trump Administration, which has struggled with constant chaos since day one. In just over one year, Trump has racked up enough controversies, feuds, and scandals that would have overcome a normal two-term presidency. He has been like a powerful storm that never blows itself out, is impossible to escape and to ignore, and is a never-ending reality show that has exhausted the nation. His supporters seemingly love him even more after the first year but a majority of Americans are afraid of another three years like the first.

The focal point of *Two Tribes*, however, is not the president himself but on how the public has and should respond to an administration like no other in history. I personally find many of his statements and actions to be indefensible and inexcusable and am baffled that most Republicans seem unable, or unwilling, to criticize him. Even more puzzling, they are seemingly embracing policies that they have found abhorrent in the past

I am a political independent and have often found the actions and positions of both parties to be, at best, lacking, and, at times, wrong. Had Hillary Clinton won, I would have had many of the same concerns. I initially intended to be equally critical of both parties but I fully acknowledge that the final result is more critical of the Republicans for two reasons: A) they control the entire government and B) Donald Trump. A traditional Republican versus Democrat analysis is insufficient, because Donald Trump has thrown much of conventional political wisdom out the window. Two centuries of political precedent, including civil discourse and principled debate, is suddenly old-fashioned, and there are apparently no rules regarding the new order except, apparently, anything that doesn't 100% support Donald Trump is marked as fake. My biggest criticism is not Trump himself but the Republicans in Congress who, for partisan gain, have thrown aside all principle, integrity, dignity, and have looked the other way. I believe that one day they will regret their acquiescence. I also believe that the second half of 2018 is a critical time in American history as we are approaching a precipice.

Where many believe that the other party's interests are a threat and that Trump in particular is a threat, how do we muster the courage to work together? We must, quite simply, work as a team. All teams, but especially a football team, are comprised of different people with different talents and weaknesses. A championship team, however, learns how to meld those diverse skills and overcome everyone's weaknesses by focusing on the common good.

Before embarking on a long season, all teams must go through the pre-season, where they focus on fundamentals. To get through the long season, with its many twists and turns, a team must rely on its offense, defense, and special teams. In a team sport like football, even the greatest superstar cannot achieve victory by himself; a team is only as good as its weakest members. While the players will all have different levels of talent and ability, championship teams find a way to merge their talents and to play as one. If the United States is to remain a championship team for decades to come, we must not allow ourselves to splinter along political and religious lines. We must strive to find common ground and find solutions to the problems that surround us. While we may not want to work with "those people" who think differently, if America wants to remain a championship team for the next generation, we have no choice.

It's easy to find fault and to blame others, to identify carnage and point the finger at others for the world's messes. It's harder to find solutions. That's what this book attempts to do. We can't solve all of our problems but we can solve many of them if we work together.

THE RULE OF FIVE

In 1993, Jack Canfield and Mark Victor Hansen had a goal: to get *Chicken Soup for the Soul* to the top of the *New York Times* bestseller's list. They realized, however, that when you can't decide which information to choose, it can cause analysis paralysis, decision fatigue, and inaction. If you don't know what to do, where do you even begin? Canfield and Hansen created *The Rule of Five:* A commitment to taking five daily actions that would quickly move their goal towards completion. The result? *Chicken Soup for the Soul* became a #1 *New York Times* bestseller and sold over 10 million copies in 39 languages.

There are so many issues and problems facing our country that sometimes we become paralyzed and don't know where to focus. With Canfield and Hansen in mind, I am adopting a political Rule of Five. For the preseason, where the emphasis is on fundamentals, this book looks at 1) partisanship, 2) truth, 3) institutions, 4) our allies, and 5) transparency.

For the long season, we examine five issues: 1) health-care, 2) our enemies, 3), climate change, 4) jobs, and 5) debt/poverty. I readily acknowledge that there are many other important issues confronting us and this list may not include your priorities. It is merely a starting point.

Lastly, to rebuild Team America and make it into a championship team, I've asked five questions: 1) Will it benefit **A**ll people, or just a few? 2) Is it **T**rue? 3) Will it be good for our **K**ids? 4) Would **J**esus approve? 5) Would Abraham **L**incoln concur?

If a decision benefits you but harms most people, I would contend that the decision or proposed law is wanting. If the only way a particular position can be sold or advanced is through exaggeration, embellishment, or by out-right lies, I would argue that deceit makes for a poor foundation. If a decision is good for me (such as tax cuts for me at the outset of the Persian Gulf War) but bad for our kids (who will have to pay for the Persian Gulf War and its deferred debt), then it is a bad decision. Lastly, would the greatest people in history support it?

To make America a championship team, we must look forward, we must act now, we must act together, and we must insist on the truth. We cannot remain two warring tribes determined to destroy the other by manipulating the truth to serve our interests. I don't care if we agree on all the details of various public policies; we have to find common ground so that solutions can be found. While Donald Trump has made things more difficult, if you are an American, you are a member of my team.

PART ONE

THE PRESEASON

1

DIVIDED

───────

"A House divided against itself cannot stand."
Abraham Lincoln

*"Any kingdom divided by civil war is doomed. A town or family splintered
by feuding will fall apart."*
Jesus, Matthew 12:25

"Say you're sorry when you hurt somebody."
All I Really Need to Know I Learned in Kindergarten

At the start of the 1978 movie *Heaven Can Wait*, Los Angeles Rams
quarterback Joe Pendleton, played by Warren Beatty, was riding his bike
and was about to be hit by a car. A rookie angel, believing that Joe's
death was imminent, swooped him up and transported him to heaven
to avoid a "mess." However, the angel received a tongue-lashing from his
supervisor because elite athlete Joe, with his superior reflexes, would have

avoided the accident. It wasn't Joe's time, the boss explained. But how to return Joe to earth?

The temporary solution was to get him into another body and recently murdered millionaire Leo Farnsworth was chosen. Joe didn't like the idea because Farnsworth was not an athlete and the Rams were close to making the playoffs. But Joe reluctantly agreed and he was returned to earth where everyone believed he was business tycoon Leo Farnsworth.

Farnsworth ruthlessly ran his businesses, resulting in endless protests and lawsuits. One day, at a company-wide board of directors meeting, Joe/Leo was baffled by the horde of angry protesters and reporters and invited them all into the meeting, to everyone's shock. Immediately, the reporters drilled the stunned board members with hostile questions about the lawsuits. Joe didn't understand what was going on and picked up some papers from a stack that showed a lawsuit involving a porpoise.

Confused, Joe said, "Some guy named porpoise is suing us?"

Board members rolled their eyes but one finally explained that they can tuna and sometimes accidentally kill some porpoises. Some people, he said, didn't like that and sued.

Joe sat back and pondered this comment while everyone in the room stared at him. After a long pause, Joe wondered that if they were a football team whether or not they would be having a winning season. The board members didn't know how to answer the question and shook their heads. Finally one spoke up and said that, overall, they had had a very good year.

"OK. We've got a winning season," Joe said excitedly, standing up. "What do you do when you're ahead? You don't make mistakes. You don't gamble unnecessarily. You protect your lead. You don't pass from your own end-zone. You make sure nobody gets hurt

'cause you got to use these guys in the next game. So, we won this game. But we got to stay in shape for the rest of the season."

While the board members and reporters were stunned, Joe/Leo continued his tirade and suggested that perhaps they could have a good guy tuna company on the porpoise team. The CFO pointed out the cost.

"We don't care how much it costs, just how much it makes," Joe exclaimed loudly. "If it costs too much, we charge a penny more. Let's be the team that makes the rules, plays fair, that gets the best contract, that's popular… We're not here for just one game. We're going all the way to the Super Bowl! And we'll already have won!"

Beatty's "porpoise speech" raised many good points that we should consider in 2018 political America. Does America have a winning team? Are we squandering our lead? Are we making sure that no one gets hurt, since we might need all of our players in the next game? Are we the team that makes the rules and plays fair? Even if we won the last game, are we in sufficient shape for the long season? Are we going to make it to the Super Bowl? Will posterity look back at us as a team for the ages?

In our hyper-partisan nation, tuna and porpoises can't work together and there are casualties. However, is it possible, as naïve Joe Pendleton asked, to have a good guy tuna company on the porpoise team? Is it possible to have a good guy Republican company on the Democratic team, or vice versa? I think it is. Even if the porpoises and tuna don't like each other, working together beats gridlock and stagnation. While the lesson of Charlottesville might be that we are hopelessly divided, the lesson of Hurricane Harvey is that Americans help each other. Given the unprecedented chaos that overwhelmed our nation in 2017, and looks to continue into the indefinite future, we need all the help we can get.

When I was about to start my junior year in college, I was, like many 20-year-olds, aimless and uncertain about my future. One night, while waiting for a friend to pick me up, I was watching the presidential debates of that year. Suddenly, I was hit by the proverbial lightning bolt and immediately knew what I was going to do with my life. I literally wrote out that night a 20 year plan after which time I would then run for political office. I decided that night that I would become a military officer, go to law school, travel the world and earn a graduate degree in international relations. I did all those things, at which time the second part of the plan kicked in: getting married and starting a family. When the 20 years had passed, however, I was knee-deep in life and to my eternal regret, I essentially abandoned my political aspirations.

But the presidential campaign of 2016 hit me like a tsunami and I became obsessed with the election and Donald Trump. I found myself following his campaign the same way someone watches a car wreck. It was appalling and yet fascinating, revolting and yet incredible. There was no way, I told myself, he would win the nomination. There was no way, I was certain, he could actually win the election. Yet on November 8, 2016, Donald J. Trump became the 45th president of the United States. Surely, I told myself, he would ultimately become presidential and govern on behalf of all Americans rather than just those who voted for him. I'm now convinced, however, that this will never happen and the result is that the country is splitting not only along ideological, racial, ethnic, and other lines but into pro-Trump and anti-Trump camps as well and is descending into tribalism. Even worse, objective truth has become a casualty in a battle between two warring tribes, being replaced by subjective and emotional truth. All that matters is how you feel, secure in the knowledge that all of your problems have been caused by the other tribe. As a result, the American team, already wracked by toxic partisanship, has been further weakened. This book examines how to rebuild the team.

Many of our leaders, and the public at large, are remaining silent and are looking the other way, excusing the inexcusable and justifying the unjustifiable. Unless we speak up, America's decline is inevitable and the nation we love will stop being great. As Winston Churchill wrote in the lead-up to World War II, *"The malice of the wicked is reinforced by the weakness of the virtuous."*[1]

A MORE PERFECT UNION

For the last two centuries, we have relied upon an incredible document called the Constitution, written by a group of 55 men with incredible foresight and vision. None would have thought in 1787 that the United States would be the richest and most powerful nation in the world in the 21st century. In 1787, the treasury was empty and the nation's debt to foreign governments, and even to its own people, could not be paid. The Confederation that had been created was impotent and was in danger of disappearing. With no money to fund an army, Congress asked the states for permission to levy a small import tax. The states said no. A short time later, Daniel Shays and a group of disgruntled farmers led a rebellion in Massachusetts and although it was put down, a great sense of fear percolated throughout the young nation.

Against this backdrop, this group met in Philadelphia to essentially overthrow the government and carry out a "bloodless coup d'etat." George Washington thought that the convention would dissolve. James Madison was afraid that the Constitution would never be ratified and Benjamin Franklin thought that with some luck, the government might last a decade. However, as a result of their brilliance, the U.S. is alive and kicking.

As a youth, I, and millions of young Americans, recited the Pledge of Allegiance before starting school each day. I used to have trouble with one word: *indivisible*. I later came to understand its meaning: that we are one nation that cannot be divided. However, this country has always been divided along many different fault lines: economically, ethnically and religiously. However, Martin Luther King declared that all Americans are linked to each other:

> *"We are tied together in the single garment of destiny, caught in the inescapable network of mutuality. And whatever affects one directly affects all indirectly. For some strange reason, you can never be what you ought to be until I am what I ought to be. This is the way God's universe is made, this is the way it is structured."* [2]

Those on the far right will never see eye to eye with those on the far left. For example, everybody agrees that "family values" are important but, as usual, the two parties have viewpoints that are diametrically opposed. As Jim Wallis wrote in *The Politics of God*:

> *"…both the Right and the Left are failing us. The Republicans' definition of family values, which properly stresses moral laxness but ignores the growing economic pressures on all families, simply doesn't go deep enough. Similarly, the Democrats are right when they focus on economic security for working families but wrong when they are reluctant to make moral judgments about the cultural trends and values that are undermining family life."* [3]

The United States has never been perfect and never will be. However, that has never been this nation's goal. The Constitution strives to be "more perfect." To comprehend the present, one must first understand the past. And if we take a quick look at the political debate that has gone back and forth over the last 200 years, finding solutions to today's problems, never an easy task, becomes slightly easier.

A PERPETUAL CYCLE

American history has shown that there is a constant ebb and flow. Emerson wrote in 1841, "*The two parties which divide the state, the party of Conservatism and that of Innovation (Liberalism), are very old and have disputed the possession of the world ever since it was made.*"[4] Arthur Schlesinger eloquently described in *The Cycles of America History* a cyclical phenomenon that swings between conservatism and liberalism, between periods of concern for the rights of the few, and periods of concern for the wrongs of the many. In the liberal periods, such as the New Deal, the object was to increase democracy, focusing on public purpose; in the conservative periods, such as the Reagan era, the goal was to contain it, concentrating on private purpose. Each epoch lasts between 20 and 30 years.

Despite George Washington's desire that political parties never develop, the philosophical battle between private interests and public purpose made partisanship inevitable and has resulted in a constant battle between the parties over the years. Alexander Hamilton's Federalist party wanted to unite the interest and credit of rich individuals with those of the state in order to foster economic growth. The Jeffersonian Republicans, in contrast, wanted to limit the intrusiveness of the federal government. For more than a century afterwards, the pendulum of political thought moved back and forth.

After the stock market crashed and the Depression began, the role of government increased under FDR and ever since, even under conservative Republicans, government has steadily increased its expansiveness. Today, virtually no aspect of society is untouched by government. However, after the war and the Depression, America embarked on a period where no party dominated. With few exceptions, the last 70 years has been dominated by political deadlock and deepening political division, resulting in what some pundits have called "the politics of parity." Consequently, the division has become increasingly cultural.

According to Jim Wallis, our public life has become a bankrupt battlefield of competing special interests without the framework of moral discourse. Since we live in a culture where the public and the media squeeze everything into two options of left and right, the goal, Wallis argues, should be to build bridges between people of goodwill in both liberal and conservative camps. And while Wallis is a devout Christian, as am I, he does not claim, nor do I, that we should strive to build a Christian government. Rather, the focus in government, he says, should be a moral compass upon which public policy is constructed.

As each side operates from its own values system and comes up with different ways of making moral judgments, the result is often emotional and contentious. Conservatives argue that moral issues of family breakdown, personal responsibility, sexual promiscuity, and substance abuse are the reasons for poverty. Liberals counter by pointing to the absence of adequate nutrition, healthcare, education, housing, and good paying jobs as keys to ending poverty. However, creating two permanently conflicting scenarios is not the solution.

As a nation, we must strive to find common ground. The way to do that, Wallis states, is to put values at the center of political discourse and in every public debate and to ask what kind of country and people we really want to be. I think that is a wise approach, but it will take political courage. Unfortunately, many people are so blinded by their allegiance to their party that they put those interests ahead of what's best for the country. John F. Kennedy, in his Pulitzer Prize-winning book *Profiles in Courage,* examined U.S. Senators that exhibited uncommon courage, placing the truth and what is right ahead of their party. He pointed out the following:

"...in Washington we are members of the Senate of the United States as well as Senators from Massachusetts and Texas. Our oath of office is administered by the vice-president, not by the governors of our respective states. We come to Washington, to paraphrase Edmund Burke, not as hostile ambassadors or special pleaders for our state or section, in opposition to advocates and agents of other areas but as members of the deliberative assembly of one nation with one interest." [5]

We need to put country ahead of party not just because it's the right thing to do, but because one-sided approaches don't work.

MANY SIDES

Sadly, both sides in the political arena often see the other side not as opponents, but as evil that can justifiably be silenced. And so in a general sense, what President Trump said in his initial response to the Charlottesville tragedy in August 2017, that "many sides" were responsible, was accurate. However, on that particular day, it was white supremacists marching with hatred in their hearts and the president should have called them out forcefully. Trump has frequently and passionately attacked others with whom he disagrees. Refugees are "animals," Mexicans are "rapists," Muslims are "terrorists," and he routinely mocked and attacked Barack Obama for failing to call Islamic radicalism by its name. But if our leaders allow this kind of evil to remain undisturbed, if they don't banish it by name from our society, those thoughts will embed themselves into our country's collective soul and bequeath a new generation of hatred.

It was unsettling that many who marched in Charlottesville wore "Make America Great Again" hats. By failing to forcefully call out the evils of bigotry, Trump emboldened those, such as David Duke, who interpreted his lack of forceful condemnation as confirmation of their hate-filled views. *The Daily Stormer*, a neo-Nazi publication, noted of President

Trump's post-Charlottesville news conference that, "*When asked to condemn, he just walked out of the room. Really, really good. God bless him.*" [6]

All presidents, until now, have tried to summon Americans to a higher moral purpose. If there's a school shooting or if a natural disaster leaves devastation, the president is supposed to express sympathy for those who suffered while providing moral comfort to the nation. Some have performed this better than others, but in his initial and third set of comments, Trump seemingly didn't even try. On a day when Nazi and KKK flags were flying, he actually talked about his trade policies and bragged that he owned a winery in Charlottesville. As the *Washington Post* wrote, Trump's trite and meandering comments were *"babble in the face of tragedy"* and *"a failure of historical imagination."* [7] Although it ended over 150 years ago, the Civil War lives on in the nation's heart and soul. This tragedy would have been an ideal opportunity to try to eradicate old ghosts that still remain, to drive a stake in the heart of evil that's still lurking, to inspire us to work together and to heal wounds that still divide us.

The only explanation for finding a moral equivalence was that Trump did not want to repudiate some of his supporters. In times of tragedy, the president must speak to the country as a whole and provide it moral clarity. Otherwise, we will be divided even further. As written in *The Hill* shortly after the tragedy, *"This is certainly no time for moral midgetry."* [8]

2017 brought several powerful hurricanes, including Harvey, one of the more powerful storms in history. The real story of Hurricane Harvey, however, was not the massive destruction, the unprecedented flooding, the rising death toll, or the millions of affected people, but the hundreds of Good Samaritans who gave their time, money, energy, heart, and even sacrificed their lives to help those who were suffering and how the entire country became Houstonians, at least for a while. The owner of several furniture stores in Houston, Jim McIngvale, known as "Mattress Mack," not only opened his storerooms to anyone needing shelter, he deployed trucks to get them, provided food, and told everyone, no matter how wet or dirty they were, that they could stay as long as they needed. Asked why he was doing it, his answer was simple.

"Black, white, brown. It doesn't matter. These are my people and I gotta help my people." [9]

This country is full of people like Mattress Mack, and we desperately need them, although many would not agree. Shortly after the election, the Southern Poverty Law Center published a report called "*The Trump Effect: The Impact of the 2016 Election on Our Nation's Schools.*" Based on a survey of more than 10,000 educators, it observed an increase in incidents involving swastikas and Nazi and Confederate Flags.[10] A teacher from Kansas wrote about how kids were saying, "Trump won, you're going back to Mexico," while a teacher from Colorado wrote about seventh-grade white boys yelling, "Heil Trump."[11] Since minorities will constitute a majority of all Americans under age 18 by 2020, these incidents are deeply disturbing.

Trump has made it clear on numerous occasions what he thinks of people of color. Haitian immigrants "*all have AIDS*" and Nigerian immigrants will never "*go back to their huts*" he said in an Oval Office meeting in June 2017 according to the *New York Times*.[12] On January 11, 2018, in a meeting with members of Congress on immigration, in reference to immigrants from places like El Salvador, Haiti, and Africa, the president shockingly said, "*Why do we want all these people from shithole countries coming here?*" Except for a few Republicans, including Rep. Mia Love, the first Haitian-American elected to Congress, who called the comments racist and demanded an apology, the silence was deafening. Even worse, a White House official told CNN, "*Though this might enrage Washington, staffers predict the comment will resonate with the base, much like his attacks on NFL players who kneel during the national anthem did not alienate it.*"[13] To top it off, the president then lied about it.

———

In many ways, this event summarized the Trump presidency. 1) He does something to divide, 2) it's often vulgar, crude, or bigoted, 3) then he lies about it, 4) Republicans give him a pass, and 5) for a public numb to the constant outrageousness, it becomes the new normal. In his thought-provoking article *"The Tragedy of President Trump's Tribalism"* in *The Atlantic*, author Ronald Brownstein addressed what he called the "coalition of restoration," the bloc of voters Trump has focused on: mostly older, blue collar, non-urban, and Evangelical whites who are uneasy about the demographic and cultural changes occurring in America. When ABC rebooted *Roseanne* in March 2018, a 1980s show about a white blue-collar family, Trump praised the show and its star, Roseanne Barr, an avid Trump supporter, and gleefully told a rally that the show was "about us." According to Brownstein, Trump has *"abandoned any pretense of seeking to represent the entire country"* and has operated in a *"uniquely tribal fashion that has ominously and, even deliberately, widened"*[14] the divides in America. His answer to the question: *In the Donald Trump era, is it possible for a deeply divided America to sustain any shared interest or common purpose?* is "it depends." It depends, he says, on whether the Republican congressional majorities will resist his divisive tendencies. However, sightings of backbones in the Republican Congress are limited and Obamacare does not cover spine transplants.

Several lawsuits have been brought alleging that Trump violated the Emoluments Clause of the Constitution by receiving money from foreign nations through his many business enterprises that might influence his actions. In December 2017, Judge George Daniels dismissed one of the cases without addressing the merits. However, his ruling raised an important issue.

"Congress is the appropriate body to determine whether, and to what extent, Defendant's conduct unlawfully infringes on that power." Judge Daniels wrote. *"Congress is not a potted plant. It is a co-equal branch of the federal government with the power to act as a body in response to Defendant's alleged*

Foreign Emoluments Clause violations, if it chooses to do so."[15] The problem is, however, that Congress chose in 2017-2018 to be a potted plant, acting only in accordance with partisan politics rather than principle, appealing only to one tribe rather than the nation as a whole.

Tribalism has existed in other countries in recent decades, including the Balkans, Beirut, and Rwanda, to mention a few, but America was always able to escape this malady, at least until recently. As Andrew Sullivan described in his insightful *New York Magazine* essay, "America Wasn't Built For Humans," this form of tribalism is ominous and foreboding:

> *"I mean a new and compounding combination of all these differences into two coherent tribes, eerily balanced in political power, fighting not just to advance their own side but to provoke, condemn and defeat the other. I mean two tribes whose mutual incomprehension and loathing can drown out their love of country, each of whom scans current events almost entirely to see if they advance not so much their country's interests but their own. I mean two tribes where one contains most racial minorities and the other is disproportionately white; where one tribe lives on the coasts and in the cities and the other is scattered across a rural and exurban expanse; where one side holds on to traditional faith and the other is increasingly contemptuous of religion altogether; where one is viscerally nationalist and the other's outlook is increasingly global; where each dominates a political party; and, most dangerously, where both are growing in intensity as they move further apart."* [16]

The result is zero-sum politics, where new administrations either desperately try to undo everything accomplished by their predecessor or achieve nothing because of gridlock. The problem with the latter is that, of course, nothing is accomplished, while the problem with the former is that politics becomes a dizzying rollercoaster where everything is thrown upside down every four years. As Sullivan points out, one of the advantages of tribalism is that you don't have to think much. All you need to know is what side you're on. Conservatives believe that "the left" is one big unified bloc of immoral, God-less socialists while liberals believe that "the right" is comprised only of fascist and intolerant white supremacists. Neither is true but the white-hot hatred created guarantees that nothing will ever be accomplished because obliteration of the other party is not a functioning philosophy for governing a nation of 300 million people.

ENOUGH!

My decision to write this book stemmed in part from my disbelief that Republicans were remaining silent in face of Trump's continuous outrageous words and actions and, for that reason, my focus is on principled Republicans who have had enough. Slowly, more and more Republicans have found the courage to speak up, including John Danforth, a Republican Senator from Missouri for 20 years as well as an ordained Episcopal priest. His blistering op-ed in the *Washington Post* on August 25, 2017 set the tone.

Danforth addressed the fact that Trump is not a conventional Republican and stated several reasons why that is the case. However, he also said, "*The fundamental reason Trump isn't a Republican is far bigger than words or policies. He stands in opposition to the founding principle of our party — that of a united country.*"[17]

Danforth reminded his readers that the first resolution of the Republican platform at the first party national convention stated that "*the union of the States must and shall be preserved*" and that Lincoln led us in a war to preserve the Union. Our Founding Fathers created a structure, he pointed out, that would accommodate within one nation all opinions and made the national motto on the presidential seal "e pluribus unum" — "*out of many, one.*" Danforth proudly listed the many times the Republican Party upheld *"the dignity of all God's people"* by building a country welcoming to all, while Trump, always eager to tell people that they don't belong, has a message of *"You are not one of us,"* the opposite of "e pluribus unum."

His concluding remarks were eye-opening:

> *"To my fellow Republicans: We cannot allow Donald Trump to redefine the Republican Party. That is what he is doing, as long as we give the impression by our silence that his words are our words and his actions are our actions...our party has been corrupted by this hateful man, and it is now in peril. In honor of our past and in belief in our future, for the sake of our party and our nation, we Republicans must disassociate ourselves from Trump by expressing our opposition to his divisive tactics..."* [18]

In the months that followed, other Republican leaders started speaking out. Senator Jeff Flake announced his retirement to his shocked colleagues on the Senate floor on October 26, 2017, while issuing a blistering diatribe against a president of his own party.

> *"We must never regard as 'normal' the regular and casual undermining of our democratic norms and ideals. We must never meekly accept the daily sundering of our country-the personal attacks, the threats against principles, freedoms and institutions, the flagrant disregard for truth or decency, the reckless provocations, most often for the pettiest and most personal reasons... Reckless, outrageous and undignified behavior has become excused and countenanced as 'telling it like it is,' when it is actually just reckless, outrageous, and undignified. And when such behavior emanates from the top of our government, it is something else: it is dangerous to democracy."* [19]

Flake followed his unprecedented speech with a scathing op-ed in the *Washington Post* the following day:

"How many more disgraceful public feuds with Gold Star families can we witness in silence before we ourselves are disgraced? How many more times will we see moral ambiguity in the face of shocking bigotry and shrug it off? How many more childish insults do we need to see hurled at a hostile foreign power before we acknowledge the senseless danger of it? How much more damage to our democracy and to the institutions of American liberty do we need to witness in silence before we count ourselves as complicit in that damage?...Enough!" [20]

Many proclaimed that the dam would now break and that all of Washington would echo the powerful words of Danforth and Flake. However, it quickly became apparent that, despite record low approval ratings for Trump, no Republican who still had to face the electorate would defy the president. Everyone ignored the moral conundrum of excusing the inexcusable and mindlessly repeated the mantra of cutting taxes as if they were all Stepford wives. The party of Lincoln has become the party of Trump.

Republicans historically were for free trade but now support Trump's imposition of tariffs in March 2018 despite a likely trade war. Republicans have generally stood for fiscal responsibility but with the $1.3 trillion budget that they passed, and Trump signed, in March 2018, the deficit will soon be over one trillion dollars and the total debt, now $21 trillion, will be increased with cumulative deficits of another $12 trillion by 2028. Republicans historically supported law enforcement but now routinely attack the FBI. Republicans used to believe that the United States was the leader of the free world and would stand up to Russia but now have apparently accepted the abdication of America's historical role as a global voice for democratic values. And Republicans used to be the party of family values but now disregard presidential lies and blindly dismiss pee tapes and porn star spankings as irrelevant.

Whatever happens as a result of the investigations into alleged collusion with Russia in the 2016 election, there can be no doubt that a hostile power tried to interfere with our election. Yet, according to a poll released on October 31, 2017 by Public Policy Polling, 79% of people who voted for President Trump say he should remain in office *even if collusion is proven!* [21]

Instead of cooperating, the Trump Administration has constantly attacked and belittled Special Counsel Robert Mueller's Russia investigation, which perhaps more than anything else, is contributing to the further widening of the two tribes. But can't we agree that it would have been wrong for a candidate to have worked hand in hand with a foreign adversary to win an election? Isn't it important to find out whether that happened or not? If it's not true, isn't exoneration a valid objective? Isn't it important to come up with a plan to make sure the Russians are not able to interfere in the future? To those who think the Russian interference is no big deal because your guy won, would you be equally nonchalant if the Russians had helped Hillary Clinton win? Does truth only matter when it's convenient or when it supports preconceived notions about the opposition? Was George Orwell correct when he pointed out that we will condone anything if done by "our side?"

Much groundwork was laid by the president and his allies in 2017 and early 2018 that Robert Mueller is biased and tainted and, consequently, any finding or recommendation that is negative towards the president, it will be argued, should be disregarded. It's hard to understand how the probe is a "partisan witch hunt" when the special counsel is a Republican, the deputy attorney general who appointed him is a Republican and Trump appointee, and the FBI director who was fired, James Comey, is a Republican appointed by a Republican president. If the Mueller probe is somehow tainted, how can the raiding of Trump's attorney's office in April 2018 by the FBI be explained, since it was carried out in New York with the approval of a Trump-appointed, and Republican, U.S.

Attorney, as well as high-level Justice Department officials and a federal judge? The FBI did not "break in," as the president claimed, and the duly executed search was not an "attack against our country." If Mueller issues a report supported by evidence and facts that demonstrates collusion or obstruction of justice, and if it is disregarded by Congress because it doesn't fit the narrative or is inconvenient for the ruling party, then November 8, 2016 will not just be a day in political history, but will specifically mark the time when tribalism became the new state religion, when truth died, when decency began its descent into oblivion, and when America's status as a superpower began to come to an end.

Mueller has for decades proven to be a dedicated public servant with impeccable credentials and he should be allowed to do his job. But both parties are making it difficult. The GOP has repeatedly pushed for a second special counsel, basically arguing that the first can't be trusted, while the Democrats filed a federal court lawsuit on April 20, 2018 against the Russian government and the Trump campaign for "unprecedented treachery." These actions will exacerbate the political divide, will further erode confidence in our judicial system and will guarantee that the fight will continue into 2019 and beyond. While imperfect, we have a system in place that we need to trust and follow the evidence wherever it may lead.

Politics will always be messy and the two sides will never totally see eye to eye. I accept that, but I don't accept the premise that politics will always be a food fight and that one must always get in the gutter to destroy the opponent. The *New York Times* reported that, before taking office, Trump told top aides to think of each presidential day as an episode in a television show where he would vanquish rivals.[22] That's not how this country works and I refuse to believe that all Trump supporters are OK with his constant vulgar and debasing insults, bragging, lying, attacking of our institutions and taking of the low road. How can a 24/7 train wreck end well? How can our nation thrive if we're always fighting? How can we expect our kids to act civilly? As Republican Senator Bob Corker told reporters in April 2018, "Continual tearing down of institutions in order to inspire your base…is damaging to our nation."[23]

Trump has constantly used the power of the presidency to divide rather than unite. In his first year in office, Trump has attacked Congress, Democrats, Republicans, Gold Star families, foreign presidents, the mayor of London, women protesters, Air Force One, the White House, Supreme Court and lower court justices, the judiciary as a whole, Chicago, Mexico, the news media, Hollywood, everybody who ran against him, the military, past presidents, Robert Mueller, NATO, our allies, Mark Cuban, the FBI, the American electoral process, the Emmys, Facebook, the intelligence agencies, Delta Airlines, Arnold Schwarzenegger, the cast of "Hamilton," the cast of "Saturday Night Live," Snoop Dogg, the pope, the Trump administration itself ("beleaguered" Jeff Sessions and the Justice Department, the IRS), Macy's, Major League baseball, Nordstrom, the Senate filibuster, the FBI, the United States of America ("You think our country's so innocent?"), the NFL and professional football players ("sons-of-bitches"), college basketball players ("I should have left them in jail"), Puerto Rico ("They want everything to be done for them"), Steve Bannon, Michael Wolff, and, incredibly, even widows of fallen soldiers. In other words, everybody except white supremacists and Vladimir Putin. He has relentlessly attacked his enemies as "sneaky," "nasty," "liddle," "sloppy," "lyin'," "Pocahontas," "Fake tears Chuck," "Jeff Flake(y)," "Al Frankenstein," "crazy," "psycho," "short and fat," "crooked," "totally inept," "a joke," "dumb as a rock," "disgusting," "puppet," "weak and out of control," "sleazy," "wacky," "totally unhinged," "incompetent," "lightweight," "the dumbest man on television," "Lamb the Sham," "low I.Q. Maxine," "sleeping son of a bitch," "Cheatin' Obama," "Slippery James Comey," "slime ball" and victim of a "bad face-lift," among others. Nearly everything he has done since he came down that escalator has been to divide "us" from "them" and attack the "fake" media.

Trump claims that he is the president who is bringing back "Merry Christmas." The truth is, however, he is the first Festivus president, the supposed holiday made famous in a Seinfeld episode that was marked by an "airing of grievances." Trump is a perpetual machine of grievances. Everybody is at fault and he, the most powerful person in the world, is the victim. And his supporters continue to give him a pass, and attack his detractors, because they support particular policies of his. But as fired FBI Director James Comey wrote,"…I don't care what your views are on immigration or taxes…A person who sees moral equivalence in Charlottesville, who talks about and treats women like they're pieces of meat, who lies constantly about matters big and small and insists the American people believe it, that person's not fit to be president of the United States on moral grounds."[24] Strong words and you may not agree. But our nation's norms and institutions are being "incinerated" like a wildfire. "It is also wrong to stand idly by, or worse, to stay silent when you know better," Comey has warned.

My wife and I have four adult children and look forward to having grandchildren. However, I cringe at the thought of having a grandchild one day ask me about the birth of tribalism and the disappearance of objective truth: "*Grandpa, how come no one did anything?*" Senator Flake's speech, and one word in particular, will be ringing in my ears. "*I have children and grandchildren to answer to, and so, Mr. President, I will not be complicit.*"[25]

Complicit. As I type this word, it sends shivers down my spine. By doing nothing, I have allowed tribalism to take hold of this country that I love. I have been complicit. By passively looking the other way, I have permitted objective truth to disappear. I have been complicit. Although I don't have all the answers, I refuse to stand idly by and be complicit anymore.

PERFECT STORM

On January 24, 2016, Trump said, "*I could stand in the middle of 5ᵗʰ Avenue and shoot somebody and I wouldn't lose voters.*" In September 2017, Representative Charlie Dent, a Pennsylvania Republican announced that he was retiring: "Before Trump, I saw the ongoing battle between what I would call the pragmatic governing wing and the purists ... Now, since Trump, the issue has become, more or less, Trump loyalty."[26] Republican Senator Bob Corker, asked about Trump supporters in March 2018 said, "...it's tribal in nature. People...don't care about issues. They want to know if you're with Trump or not."[27]

Data from Wakefield Research, as published by Fox Business on May 8, 2017, showed that couples are splitting as a result of political differences. Twenty-four percent of Americans in a relationship or married, and 42% of millennials, told the survey that "since President Trump was elected, they and their partner have disagreed or argued about politics more than ever." In fact, Wakefield found that *nearly half* of millennials who were not in a relationship would consider divorce if they had a spouse who voted for Trump.[28]

Although 2017 often looked like a runaway reality show, 2018 has resembled professional wrestling. After a relatively quiet holiday period, on his first day back in the White House on January 2, 2018, Trump demanded that a political opponent be jailed without an indictment, suggested that James Comey be locked up, insinuated that his own Justice Department was part of a Deep State plot to get him, and promised to unveil awards for the most dishonest and corrupt media. Amazingly, these were overshadowed by the president's tweet that his nuclear button was bigger than Kim Jong-Un's and issuing, after former top aide Steve Bannon accused Donald Trump, Jr. of treason, a presidential declaration that Bannon had "lost his mind." Additionally, at the stroke of midnight on January 20, 2018, on the one year anniversary of the

Trump Administration, the U.S. government shutdown, the first time ever where one party controlled both Congress and the White House. Republican Senator John McCain hit the nail on the head: *"As Republicans and Democrats run to cable news to point fingers and assign blame, the hard reality is that all of us share responsibility for this failure."*[29]

Trump accused Democrats of playing "shut-down politics" while the White House blamed it on the "behavior of obstructionist losers" and the Democrats blamed Republicans. Negotiating with the Republicans, Senator Chuck Schumer said, was like negotiating with Jell-O. Senator Tammy Duckworth, who lost both of her legs in Iraq, called the president a draft-dodger. Senator Chris Coons said dealing with the Republicans was like convincing your kids to do their homework. The White House left the following message on its answering machine: *"Thank you for calling the White House. Unfortunately, we cannot answer your call today. Congressional Democrats are holding government funding… hostage… Due to this obstruction, the government is shut down."*

The Hill concluded that our politics are broken, writing on January 20, 2018, *"the unprecedented nature of the Trump presidency is defined by the historic dysfunction present in American politics… What will perhaps define the second year of President Trump is whether the other institutions of the American economy and society can endure the division in our politics."*[30] The first year of a presidency, usually marked by optimism and the hope of a new administration, is normally when things get done, but if Trump's first year was chaotic, dysfunctional and tribalistic, is there any reasonable expectation that things will get better?

By April of 2018, Washington was, unsurprisingly, in an utter state of chaos. High-level officials continued leaving the administration at a record rate, including the secretary of state, the chief economic advisor and the national security advisor in a span of just 16 days. The new national security advisor has called for pre-emptively bombing both North Korea and Iran. Robert Mueller continued closing in on the president and began scrutinizing the Trump Organization, while the president's top personal lawyer resigned. Trump continued his assault on the FBI, the Justice and State Departments, began attacking Mueller by name and even implied that the mass school-shooting in Parkland, Florida occurred because the FBI was *"spending too much time trying to prove Russian collusion with the Trump campaign"* while others claimed that some of the students-turned-activists were actually anti-Trump "crisis actors."

The Republicans on the House Intelligence Committee wrapped up their Russia investigation without telling the Democrats and publicly disagreed with the unanimous findings of the Intelligence Community, making the entire investigation a totally political and wasteful sham. After Russia tried to kill a Russian dissident and his daughter on British soil, causing his own staff to write *"DO NOT CONGRATULATE"* on a talking points memo, the president congratulated Vladimir Putin for his election victory, drawing the wrath of John McCain: *"An American president does not lead the free world by congratulating dictators on winning sham elections."*[31] Two weeks later, the Kremlin revealed that Trump had invited Putin to the White House, something that he did not share with his aides, allies or the public.

The president found himself being further hemmed in as three different women pursued legal action against him: porn star Stormy Daniels, who claimed that Trump's attorney paid her hush-money just before the 2016 election to silence her; a Playboy center-fold, who claimed to have a lengthy affair with him; and a former contestant on the Apprentice, who claimed that the president had defamed her after he called her claims (and the claims of others) "lies."

After previously calling Attorney General's Jeff Sessions' failure to go after Trump's political opponents "disgraceful," Sessions fired Andrew McCabe, the former number two at the FBI, 26 hours before he was due to retire, prompting Trump to call it a *"great day for democracy."* Former CIA Director John Brennan's response was breath-taking. *"When the full extent of your venality, moral turpitude and political corruption becomes known, you will take your rightful place as a disgraced demagogue in the dustbin of history."*[32] As one commentator put it, "It's a race to the bottom."[33]

Trump stunned advisors in March as he accepted on-the-spot an invitation to meet with North Korea's Kim Jong-Un, following a seemingly out-of-the-blue decision to slap tariffs on steel and aluminum, and later against Chinese goods, resulting in retaliation by China. Without consulting the Pentagon, the president announced in April of 2018 that the U.S. military would be used at the border until "the Wall" was complete and would pull out of Syria. These shoot from-the-hip decisions angered allies, confused the public, spooked the stock market, raised the prospect of a trade war and many, including John McCain, blamed Syria's chemical attacks against the rebels in April on Trump's sudden decision to leave Syria. Although the U.S. later retaliated with a missile strike, the president seemed unable to criticize Syria's key ally, Russia. When U.N. Ambassador Nikki Haley publicly announced further sanctions against Russia, she was called "confused" and the president personally intervened to halt sanctions.

In a special election in Pennsylvania in March 2018, while stumping for the Republican, Trump held a rally and further perpetuated the idea of a "Deep State" controlling Washington and victimizing him. *"There is a lot of evil. A lot of bad people."* In an election that sent shock waves through the Republican party, Democratic newcomer Conor Lamb won in a district Trump carried by 20 points in 2016.

After conservative backlash for the $1.3 trillion budget bill, which included virtually nothing towards a "big, beautiful Wall," Trump lashed out with a series of harsh tweets to rally his base ("Our country is being stolen") and falsely stated on March 23 that construction on the Wall would be starting on "Monday" (March 26). Since funds earmarked for border protection construction and improvements can only be used to repair and build previously approved fencing, that statement was not true although "Build the Wall" definitely sounds stronger than "Repair the Fence." Trump tried to have it both ways; on April 5, he bragged that border crossings were at a 46-year low but that sending troops to the border was necessary, causing many to argue that he was creating an emergency that did not exist to placate angry supporters like Ann Coulter. "*They don't call it the Great Tweet of China*," Coulter said, mocking Trump's constant tweeting instead of actually building the Wall as he had promised.

Most believe that after the passage of the $1.3 trillion budget in March, nothing further will be accomplished for the remainder of the year due to the mid-term elections. Although seven months of inaction by our leaders is a sad indictment of our system, "trillion dollar deficits and no Wall" is hardly a winning slogan. Accordingly, many conservatives fear a possible blue wave, where Democrats regain the House and possibly even the Senate, especially with Speaker of the House Paul Ryan's decision to retire. If that happens, any hope Trump will have of enacting his agenda will come to a screeching halt and investigations and impeachment proceedings will be certain to follow. Trump's only apparent courses of action will be to create hysteria ("Stop the massive inflow of Drugs and People") or change the subject by falsely attacking a successful company (Amazon) for not paying taxes (it does) and cheating the Post Office (it doesn't). Instead of leadership and legislation, we will no doubt see more lashing out and lying until the elections, resulting in a further poisoning of the system and greater tribalism.

With this chaos as the backdrop, a perfect storm erupted in Washington as summer of 2018 approached. Former George W. Bush official Richard Haass called it the "*most perilous time in modern American history*" as Trump was "*now set for wars on three different fronts*"-political (Mueller), economic (trade war) and actual (North Korea and Iran).[34] Mix all of those together, add a cornered, unpredictable and combustible president with a depleted staff, a porn star, an all-out assault on institutions, and likely losses in November, and a positive outcome is hard to visualize. Since Trump has consistently tried to criminalize and dehumanize his political opponents, negotiation and political compromise with Democrats has become nearly impossible. The only thing that could avert the coming tsunami is if Republican leaders put country over party. That seems unlikely, however. As Republican Congressman Trey Gowdy, one of several dozen House Republicans who are retiring said in April 2018, *"We've convinced ourselves that we have to (win) because the country will go to Hades in a handbasket if my team doesn't win."*[35] As the two parties strive to "win," the country, unfortunately, will lose.

LANCE ARMSTRONG AND CARSON WENTZ

The second half of 2018 is a critical time in U.S. history. Republicans have hitched their fortunes to Donald Trump and will most likely stay with Trump until the bitter end. The Democrats will likely regain power in November and impeach the president, as the Republicans did to Bill Clinton. But since it's doubtful that 67 senators will vote to remove him from office, as with Clinton, the entire spectacle will be an expensive, nation-draining waste of time that will further divide us and embolden our enemies. A president has never been removed from office in American history and unless done in a bipartisan fashion, the country as a whole will suffer.

In 1973, a special committee in Congress was created to investigate the Watergate scandal. The committee of four Democrats and three Republicans issued a bipartisan final report on June 27, 1973 that detailed its findings on presidential "corruption, fraud and abuse of official powers." One Republican, Lawrence Hogan of Maryland, father of Maryland's current governor, said, "It is impossible for me to condone the long train of abuses to which [Nixon] has subjected the presidency and the people of this country."[36]

Such bipartisanship seems almost quaint today. So what's the answer? The solution is to look to sports, which is, in many ways, the only "true" thing that exists in life. Everything else is spun. From the courtroom to the boardroom to the pulpit to the government, spinning has become the national pastime. But in sports, somebody wins and somebody loses. All Americans are on the same team. Teammates sometimes call each other out and sometimes teammates praise and support each other. The key, however, is what's best for the team.

Lance Armstrong, the seven-time winner of the Tour De France, denied for years that he was involved in doping, but the world of the planet's most famous cyclist came crashing down when 11 of his former teammates finally spoke up. Travis Tygart, chief executive of the U.S. Anti-Doping Agency said, "*It took tremendous courage for the riders on the U.S. Postal Service team and others to come forward and speak truthfully. It is not easy to admit your mistakes and accept your punishment. But that is what these riders have done for the good of the sport.*"[37] Armstrong's teammates spoke up and that's what Congress must do for the "good of the nation."

On February 4, 2018, the Philadelphia Eagles won their first Super Bowl 41-33 over the New England Patriots. Most experts believed that the Patriots, five-time Super Bowl winners, led by the greatest quarterback ever, Tom Brady, had more talent. Eagles franchise quarterback Carson Wentz had been heading towards an MVP award for his outstanding play during the 2017 season but a serious injury sent him to the sideline and catapulted journeyman Nick Foles into the limelight. As Foles became a national hero, Wentz enthusiastically praised and supported his teammate without any jealousy whatsoever. "*God is so good!!!! World Champions!!!! So proud of this team!!!! Told y'all my boy @Nfoles_9 was gonna shine tonight! Well deserved my bro!*" Wentz tweeted afterwards.[38]

To get to the Super Bowl, we must work as a team. Like Carson Wentz, we have to not care who gets the credit and, like Lance Armstrong's teammates, we have to speak up when something's wrong. In the Sermon on the Mount, Jesus issued the following advice: *"Why worry about a speck in your friend's eye when you have a log in your own?...First get rid of the log in your own eye; then you will see well enough to deal with the speck in your friend's eye."* Democrats and Republicans have different philosophies regarding government and society but we're on the same team. Let's take the logs out of our eyes and work together.

We live in the greatest country in the world. At some point, however, people will start knocking down the walls of our divided house and, if we are not careful, it will collapse. The solution lies in the future and with all of us, with our imperfections and flaws, putting country ahead of party, insisting on truth, using the principles of Lincoln and the words of Jesus, and working as a team for the benefit of every single American so that our kids will inherit a better world than we did. We must unite when there is division, speak up when our government fails us, insist on the truth, put country ahead of party and be indivisible when there is a crisis. Our nation has devolved into two warring tribes, lying to justify their position. That needs to change. Do you want to get to the Super Bowl? I do too, but the only way to get to there is to play as a team. If we do that, our best days are ahead of us, not behind us.

2

TRUTH

―――――

"God cannot be for and against the same thing at the same time."
Abraham Lincoln

"The words you say will either acquit you or condemn you."
Jesus, Matthew 12:37

"Play fair."
All I Really Need to Know I Learned in Kindergarten

Having lived in San Diego for the last 35 years, I became a huge San Diego Chargers fan (don't get me started on the 2017 decision to move the team to Los Angeles). On May 2, 2012, one of the greatest Chargers of all-time, All-Pro linebacker Junior Seau, having recently retired after a 20-year career, shot himself at the age of 43. The entire city of San Diego was in shock trying to make sense of this tragedy and thousands grieved like they had lost a family member.

―――――

Seau, it was later revealed, suffered a type of brain injury resulting from repeated shots to the head during his NFL career. As it turns out, he wasn't the only one.

In 1994, the NFL acknowledged the danger of concussions for the first time, but its Mild Traumatic Brain Injury ("MTBI") Committee downplayed it, telling *Sports Illustrated, "Concussions are part of the profession, an occupational risk."*[1] In 2002, Dr. Bennet Omalu (played by Will Smith in the 2015 movie *Concussion*) noticed a splotchy accumulation of tau protein in the brain of former Pittsburgh Steeler Mike Webster, evidence of a brain disease that Omalu called Chronic Traumatic Encephalopathy, or CTE. In 2005, Omalu wrote about his conclusions regarding Webster's brain in the journal *Neurosurgery.*[2] The MTBI committee attacked his report and demanded that *Neurosurgery* retract the article.

Despite mounting evidence, in 2007, Dr. Ira Casson, co-chairman of the MTBI, said in an interview that there was no link between head injuries and depression, dementia, early onset Alzheimer's, or "any long-term problems." The following year, an NFL-commissioned survey found former players suffered Alzheimer's and dementia at a rate 19 times higher than for non-players between the ages of 30-49. The NFL called the study "inconclusive."[3]

Over the next few years, nearly 250 cases, with 5,000 plaintiffs, were filed by former players against the NFL, including former players from the 1940s. A year after Seau's death, the lawsuits were settled, with the NFL paying out $765 million without admitting liability.

"Commissioner Goodell and every owner gave the legal team the same direction," NFL counsel Jeff Pash said, speaking after the settlement. *"Do the right thing for the game and for the men who played it."*[4]

"Do the right thing" seems like sound advice. Unfortunately for the NFL, it took twenty years of denials and numerous deaths to do the right thing and acknowledge the truth. As Jesus once said, "the truth will set you free," but the 2016 election and the Trump presidency so far has sadly shown us that the truth is a diminishing commodity in partisan America.

REALITY IS IRRELEVANT

The Oxford Dictionary selected "post-truth" as its 2016 Word of the Year, defining it as, "*Relating to or denoting circumstances in which objective facts are less influential in shaping public opinion than appeals to emotion and personal belief.*"[5] In a post-truth world, feelings become fact. Trump's "truth" comes from his own gut feelings and life experiences and his devoted supporters accept his truth without question. This apparently means, sadly, that truth is no longer the fundamental building block of decision-making in America. The fact that all 17 U.S. intelligence organizations, including both the FBI and the CIA, affirmed that Russia intervened in the 2016 election in part to help Donald Trump win the White House, for example, is meaningless to Trump and his supporters since they have other convictions.

On October 24, 2017, Republican Senator Bob Corker, who was considered for both vice-president and secretary of state, gave a stunning interview with CNN and said, after Trump tweeted that Corker had begged for his endorsement and couldn't get elected dog-catcher, the following about the president:

> "*I would hope the staff over there would figure out ways of controlling him when they know that everything he said today was absolutely untrue.*"

> "*Unfortunately, I think world leaders are aware that much of what he says is untrue. Certainly, people here are because these things are provably untrue. They're just factually incorrect.*"

"At the end of the day, when his term is over, I think the debasing of our nation — the constant non-truth telling, the name-calling — I think the debasement of our nation is what he'll be remembered most for." [6]

Even more damning, on the Senate floor in January 2018, Republican Senator Jeff Flake called Trump's use of the term "enemy of the people" shameful and repulsive and compared it to Soviet dictator Joseph Stalin. *"2017 was a year,"* the senator said, *"which saw the truth –objective, empirical, evidence-based truth – more battered and abused than any other time in the history of our country, at the hands of the most powerful figure in our government."* The senator added, *"For without truth, and a principled fidelity to truth and to shared facts, Mr. President, our democracy will not last."* [7] Such language from the Senate floor is unprecedented.

Every era has its own definition of "truth." The Victorians believed that it emanated from God. When wars were fought, your side won because you had "truth" on your side. Belief in truth went hand in hand with faith in institutions, the implication being that society would make moral and economic progress simultaneously. The carnage of World War I pulled the rug out from under that premise while Vietnam further undermined the authority and credibility of government, its institutions, and the notion of "truth."

Although Jimmy Carter promised to never lie to us, almost all presidents have lied. In 1964, Congress passed the Gulf of Tonkin Resolution giving President Johnson authority to escalate the Vietnam war, based on information he provided that was false. In 1985, Iran offered to free hostages in exchange for weapons. The Reagan Administration hatched a plan where Israel would ship missiles to Iran, the U.S. would resupply Israel with the missiles, and the U.S. would receive the cash that had been paid. That cash would then go to Nicaragua, to fund the *contras*, who were fighting to take down the elected Sandinista government. Reagan told the public that, "*We did not, I repeat, did not trade weapons or anything else [to Iran] for hostages, nor will we*" but a few months later he admitted the truth.

Early in 1961, President Kennedy stated, "*I have previously stated, and I repeat now, that the United States plans no military intervention in Cuba*" but just a few months later, Cuban nationals, backed by the CIA, invaded Cuba. In 1940, Franklin Roosevelt ran for reelection as a peace candidate. "*I have said this before, but I shall say it again and again and again: Your boys are not going to be sent into any foreign wars,*" he told voters. Even as he made his assurances, he was secretly meeting with Winston Churchill to plot ways to provide Great Britain with badly needed arms. Eisenhower denied that U2 spy planes were flying over the Soviet Union when they were, Bush 41 said "*Read my lips. No new taxes,*" before taxes were imposed and Bill Clinton famously said, "*I did not have sexual relations with that woman, Miss Lewinsky.*" None of them, however, could compare to Richard Nixon, who set the gold standard for presidential lying. However, even Tricky Dick couldn't hold a candle to Donald Trump.

Over the past 20 years, the proliferation of political talk shows and the rise of the internet have created a fragmented media environment where people tend to live in bubbles. Since there is no one specific media gatekeeper, politicians are able to lie more easily. In an era of hyper-partisanship, where politicians try to court the most loyal voters at the extreme ends of the political spectrum, they often lie without consequences, despite the rise of fact-checking websites. Because of the unrelenting attack by Team Trump against the "Fake media," he can not only get away with his mountain of lies, many supporters don't realize they are not true.

On June 23, 2017, the *New York Times* published an article bluntly titled "*Trump's Lies*" and made the following incredible comments:

"Every president has shaded the truth or told occasional misstatements. No other president of either party has behaved as Trump is behaving. He is trying to create an environment in which reality is irrelevant... we believe his long history of using untruths to serve his purposes, as a businessman and politician, means that his statements are not simply careless errors. We are using the word 'lie' deliberately. Not every falsehood is deliberate on Trump's part but it would be the height of naivete to imagine he is merely making honest mistakes. He is lying." [8]

While truth is often in the eye of the beholder, and liberals and conservatives see the world differently, I am not talking about subjective topics where opinions vary, but rather factual matters where opinions are irrelevant. You can't say my name is Fred because my name is Jim.

The *Washington Post* reported that as of January 19, 2018, after one year in office, Trump had made more than 2000 false statements, *an average of more than five per day.*[9] The project was originally meant to end after Trump's first 100 days but was extended to one year by popular demand. In a January 2, 2018 article, the *Post* acknowledged that because it lacked resources and staff, it might discontinue the project.[10] Think about that. One of the country's largest papers doesn't have the resources to monitor the president's lies.

Of the 2000 plus lies, the following one is illustrative. Immediately after the terrorist act in Barcelona on August 17, 2017, where over 100 people were injured by an automobile deliberately running people down, President Trump challenged the world to *"study what General Pershing of the United States did to terrorists when caught,"* adding in his Twitter post, *"There was no more radical Islamic terror for 35 years!"*

During the 2016 campaign, Trump claimed that Gen. John J. Pershing had crushed a rebellion in a Muslim province of the Philippines after the Spanish-American War. Supposedly, he captured "50 terrorists" and shot all but one with bullets smeared in pig's blood. The survivor was ordered to spread the tale of the episode. *"And for 25 years, there wasn't a problem."* Despite his 2017 tweet adding10 years to the claim, *"This is a repeated myth that has no basis in truth,"* said James R. Arnold, the author of *Moro War: How America Battled a Muslim Insurgency in the Philippine Jungle, 1902-1913.*[11] Numerous other historians concur. Trump has never offered any evidence. Therefore, in response to an international terrorist incident, the message the president of the United States asked the world to "study" was a lie.

Think about that.

Of course, his political career was started on a lie when he accused Barack Obama of not being born in America, a lie that he did not disavow until late 2016, at which time he falsely accused Hillary Clinton of starting it and patted himself on the back by "ending it."

No one knows the truth regarding the allegations of sexual harassment of 20 plus women against the president and I am not sure we will ever know. But since he has lied about nearly everything else, the odds are that he is lying when he says all of the women are lying. Trump angrily claimed that Michael Wolff's salacious book *Fire and Fury* was "full of lies," prompting Wolff to reply that Trump is *"a man who has less credibility than, perhaps, anyone who has ever walked on earth,"* an ordinarily wild statement that is in this case hard to refute.

Many of Trump's lies are admittedly trivial, such as holding the record for being on the cover of *Time* Magazine the most, or claiming that he was responsible for there being no airline fatalities in 2017. Some are simply ridiculous, such as the bowling ball justification for the March 2018 decision to impose tariffs on steel and aluminum. "It's called the bowling ball test…they (Japan) take a bowling ball from 20 feet up and drop it on the hood of the car. And if the hood dents, the car doesn't qualify. It's horrible, the way we're treated."

Many lies would be overlooked if he didn't keep repeating them. On over 50 occasions, including in his State of the Union speech, Trump boasted that the 2017 tax bill was the largest in history even though Treasury Department data shows that it would rank eighth. Trump has falsely claimed over 25 times that the U.S. pays the highest amount of corporate taxes in the world and that the U.S. is one of the highest taxed nations in the world. Neither is true.

He repeatedly embellishes his accomplishments. "*We have more legislation passed, including – the record was Harry Truman a long time ago, and we broke that record, so we got a lot done,*" Trump said to fire-fighters over the Christmas holiday in 2017. However, an analysis by GovTrack, a web site that tracks bills in Congress, shows that Trump had signed the fewest bills into law at this point than any president in more than 60 years, back to Eisenhower.[12]

Other lies, like Trump's false claim that millions of undocumented immigrants had cast ballots for his opponent in the 2016 election, pose a threat, scholars say, since his administration may actually build policies around them. As discussed further in chapter three, a survey taken in August 2017 by the *Washington Post* showed that more than half of Republicans surveyed were OK with a proposed plan to postpone the 2020 election until the U.S. "*figured out how to deal with wide-spread voter fraud.*"[13] Even more serious, at a March 2018 fundraiser, Trump admitted to donors lying to Canadian Prime Minister Justin Trudeau about whether the U.S. had a trade surplus with Canada (it doesn't). "Wrong, Justin. You do. I didn't even know…I had no idea. I just said, 'you're wrong.'"[14] Aside from not knowing whether or not there was a trade deficit, lying to a foreign leader, and then bragging about it, destroys American credibility.

Despite the presence of fact checkers who have pointed out *thousands* of falsehoods and outright lies by the president, many believe that Trump is delivering a different kind of truth-an emotional truth. Tom Forman, chief executive of reality shows like *Extreme Makeover: Home Edition*, pointed out that Trump is a master of being "directionally correct," amplifying what people already know "in their bones" to be true.[15] Since psychologists frequently tell us that most people make decisions based on feelings rather than facts, it shouldn't be shocking that emotional truth "trumps" factual truth.

But if everything is emotional and subjective, then everything depends and nothing is absolute. One of the main tenets of Christianity is that there are absolute truths. Few things irritate a strong Christian more than the concept of relative truth. However, with Trump, everything becomes relative and nothing is absolute. Moreover, if the president can lie with impunity, then so can senators, judges, prosecutors, professors, employers, doctors, teachers, coaches, and students. Where does it end?

WORDS DEFILE

Before Jesus was crucified, he was brought before Pilate and said to the Roman governor "*I was born and came into the world to testify to the truth. All who love the truth recognize that what I say is true.*" Pilate cynically retorted, "*What is truth?*"

Truth, some would say, is subjective and varies from person to person. It shouldn't be like that, but not everyone sees the world the same way nor does everyone agree on the truth. If you want to know, for example, whether Bill Clinton or Donald Trump obstructed justice, you would need to look at the evidence and the applicable statute to decide. But why then did every Democrat conclude in Clinton's 1999 impeachment trial that he did not obstruct justice as charged while nearly every Republican did? And why did nearly every Democrat in 2017 say that Trump obstructed justice when he fired James Comey when nearly every Republican said he did not? Why did the vast majority of white people think in 1995 that O.J. Simpson was guilty while the vast majority of black people did not? If you are seeking the truth, what difference does one's political party or race make? Truth is truth, right?

The majority of Trump's factual misstatements have been belligerent, juvenile and mean attacks, insults and put-downs. No matter what your party, age, race, or occupation, this cannot be defended for, as Jesus stated so eloquently, it is the words a man speaks that defiles him.

> *"Then Jesus called to the crowd to come and hear. 'Listen,' he said, 'and try to understand. It's not what goes into your mouth that defiles you; you are defiled by the words that come out of your mouth'… Then Peter said to Jesus, 'Explain to us the parable that says people aren't defiled by what they eat.'*
>
> *"'Don't you understand yet?' Jesus asked. 'Anything you eat passes through the stomach and then goes into the sewer. But the words you speak come from the heart — that's what defiles you. For from the heart come evil thoughts, murder, adultery, all sexual immorality, theft, lying, and slander. These are what defile you.'"* (Matthew 15, 10-20)

The Bible mentions honesty, truth, and integrity 271 times and it is clear that these concepts are important to God. The prophet Jeramiah recorded that God said to him, "*Run up and down every street in Jerusalem. Look high and low, search throughout the city! If you can find one just and honest person, I will not destroy the city. But even when they are under oath, saying, 'As surely as the Lord lives,' they are still telling lies.*" Jeramiah 5: 1-2 (NLT).

And yet, to my eternal astonishment, some of Trump's most vocal supporters are Christians. Christian pastor Johnny Enlow, who is also an author and international speaker, wrote, in relevant part, the following in May of 2017: "*Last night I was awakened with an intense and fiery word from the Lord that I will attempt to convey. This is what I heard:*

"Be not moved and shaken by the present shakings, rumblings and reactions coming out of DC. I did not go out of My way to affect this last election to then suddenly have it aborted. I played My Trump card and I will win the hand… I chose Trump for purposes you must yet be patient to watch for. The hordes of Hell in media have rallied in mass under Leviathan but I will crush them under the forces that I have released under My trusted archangel Gabriel. He will be instrumental in devastating media outlets that do not position themselves as lovers of truth and goodness. There will be in-house fires that will not be able to be put out in some major media outlets. There will be the hanging by the very noose they have created for others… My Trump card is something I will continue to play." [16]

As a Christian, it is not easy for me to read a Christian pastor who says that God will crush the "hordes of hell in media" and will devastate media outlets that criticize the president by playing his "Trump card." And while I have no doubt that Pastor Enlow's beliefs are sincere, I refuse to live in Trump's wonderland, where everything he says is supposedly true while whatever anybody says that is negative or critical of him is false and fake. I will take exception to those who blindly support him, including my fellow followers of Jesus Christ.

I will support and pray for Trump if he acts honorably, but if he acts in such a way that is harmful to this great country, I will speak up because words defile and truth matters. Instead of cowering in silence, I hope others will join me, whether Democrat or Republican, Christian, Jew or Muslim. Lying by our leaders harms us all, including future generations; it creates further divisions, it makes a mockery of our rule of law, it exposes our government to charges of hypocrisy, it reduces our influence and reputation in the global community, it is an offense to the commands of God and the words of Jesus, and Lincoln, if alive today, would be embarrassed.

We can't just look the other way and allow a new normal to take over our lives where truth doesn't matter. We must not become so numb to this reckless reality show that we simply say "whatever" nor can we blindly justify perpetual lies because they're coming from a member of our tribe. Objective truth matters and words defile. A post-truth society is one step away from anarchy. As Senator Flake ominously warned, "*If we compromise the truth for the sake of our politics, we are lost.*" If you believe that whatever Trump says or does is alright because you voted for him or are a member of his party, or because you believe that any Republican who challenges the president is a traitor, I will not argue but will merely quote Edmund Burke:

"All that is necessary for the triumph of evil is for good men to do nothing."

3

FAKE!

─────────

"*I am not bound to win, but I am bound to be true. I am not bound to succeed, but I am bound to live by the light that I have. I must stand with anybody that stands right, and stand with him while he is right, and part with him when he goes wrong.*"
Abraham Lincoln

"*Hypocrite! First get rid of the log in your own eye; then you will see well enough to deal with the speck in your friend's eye.*"
Jesus, Matthew 7:5

"*Don't hit people.*"
All I Really Need to Know I Learned in Kindergarten

In 1998, after an abysmal year, the San Diego Chargers had the number one draft pick. A vigorous debate broke out between whether they should draft Peyton Manning, the star quarterback from Tennessee, or

Ryan Leaf, the muscular star out of Washington State. The Chargers selected Leaf who arguably became the biggest bust in sports history. Manning became a Hall of Famer with the Colts and one of the greatest quarterbacks in NFL history.

After the Colts had set up a meeting at the NFL Combine, Leaf never arrived. It was a sign of things to come. When the Colts got a look at Leaf at the weigh-in, he turned them off again. Leaf stepped onto the scale, twenty pounds overweight, and with the camera flashes popping in his face, flexed his biceps. "*It was clear that Ryan hadn't prepared for the Combine, even though he should have viewed it as one of the most important events, and opportunities, of his life. Ryan couldn't have made a worst first impression,*" said a witness.

The Chargers ended up drafting Leaf and, at first, he seemed like the real deal. The Colts and Chargers met in the 1998 preseason and the Chargers rolled to a 33-3 victory. However, through the grapevine it quickly spread that Leaf was a complete jerk and had zero respect in the San Diego locker room. By the time the Chargers set out for Indianapolis in Week 5, Leaf had already cursed out a camera man, launched into an obscenity-filled tirade against a reporter, and been booed by the San Diego fans. Things never got better and after his short NFL career, Leaf was sentenced to prison after pleading guilty to felony burglary and drug possession charges.

The Bible tells us that man looks at the outside of a person while God looks at the heart. Many were sold on Leaf because of his physical strengths and overlooked that he was selfish and had no heart. He was supposed to be the Chargers savior but he was, simply put, fake news.

ASSAULT ON INSTITUTIONS

The 2016 election was dominated by something completely new to politics: fake news. The reasons for this phenomenon are multi-faceted, but since Trump's election we have seen an assault on our institutions like never before in history. Such an assault has long-term implications for our country that will last far beyond a Trump Administration.

President Trump used the word "fake" more than 400 times during the first year of his presidency. Interestingly, he never talked about "fake news" even once during his campaign but now that phrase, perhaps more than any other, has come to summarize his administration. A January 2018 study by Gallup and the Knight Foundation showed that "*forty percent of Republicans say accurate news stories that cast a negative light should always be considered fake news.*"[1]

The media, we're told, cannot be trusted. CNN, NBC, CBS, ABC, the *Washington Post*, and the *New York Times*, along with others, are "fake news." During a joint press conference with the President of Latvia on April 3, 2018, President Trump told President Vejonis to pick a "Baltic reporter" to ask a question. "*A Baltic reporter ideally. Real news, not fake news.*"

The president's supporters have taken up his mantra that the mainstream media is nothing but fake news. A Monmouth University poll released in April 2018 found three out of every four Americans think traditional media publishes "fake news."[2] This non-stop assault on our institutions damages our nation's long-term interests. The media plays a critical role in insuring that government does not overstep its bounds so that freedom and democracy can thrive. However, the administration seems determined to diminish the media's influence by denigrating it at every chance and even calling it the "enemy of the people." The president's New Year's Eve tweet was chilling:

> "*As our Country rapidly grows stronger and smarter, I want to wish all of my friends, supporters, enemies, haters, and even the very dishonest Fake News Media, a Happy and Healthy New Year. 2018 will be a great year for America!*"

While there is no doubt that totally untrue stories have appeared in the media, all credibility is lost when everything is falsely proclaimed to be fake. After his campaign manager was indicted on October 30, 2017 and a former aide pleaded guilty for lying to the FBI about attempts by the Trump campaign to get "dirt" on Hillary Clinton from the Russians, Trump tweeted as follows on October 31, 2017:

> *"The Fake News is working overtime. As Paul Manafort's [sic] lawyer said, there was 'no collusion' and events mentioned took place long before he came to the campaign. Few people knew the young, low level volunteer named George, who has already proven to be a liar. Check the DEMS!"*

However, the "Fake News" did not falsely report that George (Papadopoulos) had pleaded guilty. He actually did! Republican Senator Flake emotionally pointed out how destructive this tendency to wrongly call things that are true fake and things that are fake true in his speech on the Senate floor in October 2017:

> *"We were not made great as a country by indulging or even exalting our worst impulses, turning against ourselves, glorying in the things which divide us and calling fake things true and true things fake."* [3]

The all-out war with the media also has international implications and can create serious harm in foreign policy. In December 2017, CNN did a report about slavery in Libya but the Libyan government tried to discredit the report as "fake news," using President Trump's repeated assertions in its defense. By maliciously attacking the press and journalists, Trump, perhaps unwittingly, gives cover to foreign despots. Senator John McCain, in an op-ed in the *Washington Post* on January 17, 2018, pointed out the global ramifications of shouting "fake" at everything:

"The phrase 'fake news' – granted legitimacy by an American president – is being used by autocrats to silence reporters, undermine political opponents, stave off media scrutiny, and mislead citizens," McCain said. "The Committee to Protect Journalists documented 21 cases in 2017 in which journalists were jailed on 'fake news' charges. Trump's attempts to undermine the free press also make it more difficult to hold repressive governments accountable." [4] This is a senior Republican senator.

However, the assault on our institutions, unfortunately, has been extended far beyond the media and can serve no constructive purpose.

Federal court judges previously nominated by other presidents, and confirmed by the Senate, became "so-called" judges.

Trump pardoned controversial sheriff Joe Arpaio in August 2017 for criminal contempt, after Arpaio repeatedly disobeyed a federal court judge before the sentence had even been imposed. This brazen act, done without consultation with the Justice Department, clearly conveyed that judges you disagree with don't have to be obeyed.

The intelligence community, comprised of 17 agencies, was likened to Nazi Germany.

The appointment of a special counsel to investigate Russian meddling is a "witch-hunt" even though Robert Mueller, the highly respected former FBI director who served a Republican and Democratic president, was appointed by Trump's own Justice Department.

NATO, we've been told, is obsolete.

Former President Obama became a "sick or bad guy" and "Cheatin' Obama."

Trump has repeatedly insisted that the Senate rewrite its parliamentary rules, even though virtually no senator agrees, oblivious to the fact that such a short-sighted action would hurt Republicans when Democrats inevitably regain power one day.

Trump tweeted that Comey better not leak to the press because he might have tapes, a charge that Trump admitted was fantasy six weeks later. Ironically, this tweet caused Comey to leak his memo of his meeting with Trump, which led to the appointment of a special counsel.

On July 2, 2017, Trump tweeted a video of him wrestling with and punching a figure that had the CNN logo superimposed on its head.

The Congressional Budget Office (CBO), the independent, non-partisan highly respected agency that analyzes the impact of legislative proposals, can't be trusted, the president said.

It was reported in June 2017 that at least five of Trump's clubs, from South Florida to Scotland, a framed photo of Trump on the cover of *Time* Magazine was displayed. The cover, dated March 1, 2009, has a stern picture of Trump, arms crossed, that says, "*Donald Trump: The Apprentice is a television smash!*" Across the top of the cover it says, "*Trump is hitting on all fronts... Even TV!*" Just one problem. It was fake. *Time* has confirmed that no such magazine cover was ever published on that date with that photo.

In late July 2017, President Trump launched a "real news" video series on his Facebook page, part of his longstanding effort to dismiss the "fake" news of the mainstream media. Some said the video series "*smacks of the kind of thing that was done in Nazi Germany*" while former U.S. Ambassador to Russia Michael McFaul tweeted that the video felt like "state-owned channels."[5] Political spinning is nothing new but this "real news" should cause some concern, since its main goal seems to be discrediting the mainstream media.

In December 2017, the president asserted in a *New York Times* interview that he had the "absolute right to do what I want to do with the Justice Department." Leaving aside the apparent reckless belief the president has that he can direct government investigations himself and that people can be jailed without indictments or trials, the repeated claim of a "Deep State" that is out to get him has the potential to do irreversible damage. When HUD Secretary Ben Carson got in hot water in March of 2018 for ordering a $31,000 dining room table for his office, New York Republican Congresswoman Claudia Tenney claimed that someone in the "Deep State" had ordered the table to embarrass the administration.[6] And many in Congress have been calling for the appointment of a second special counsel to investigate the FBI because, as Congressman Steve Scalise has argued, "it's the only way to ensure the public has full faith in Mueller's findings."[7] A March 2018 Monmouth University poll found that 74% of Americans believe in a Deep State while a SurveyMonkey poll for Axios showed in February 2018 that nearly 50% of Republicans have an unfavorable view of the FBI.[8] But constant attacks on our government, by the leaders of the government, only causes further distrust and cynicism.

One of President Trump's most outrageous assertions has been that he would have won the popular vote had 3 to 5 million "illegals" not voted in the 2016 election. While such claims of large-scale voter fraud are false, a survey reported by the *Washington Post* on August 10, 2017 suggests that about half of Republicans would support postponing the 2020 presidential election until the country can fix this problem.[9] While the survey was only measuring reactions to a hypothetical situation, the results are staggering. Fake news is not only prevalent, it works, and that is incredibly scary.

It seems that the president conflates the government with himself and sees everything through an extremely personal prism. In his mind, he is the United States. In a January 2018 interview with the *Wall Street Journal*, the president said that Peter Strzok, the FBI counter-intelligence agent who was kicked off Mueller's team for texting anti-Trump messages, had committed "treason." When NFL players kneel during the National Anthem, they are disrespecting him. He seems to believe that everybody in government works for him. However, the job of the attorney general, or the director of the FBI, or members of the U.S. Senate is to represent and defend the people of the United States, not to protect the president.

The thing that makes tribalism so dangerous is that you apparently must also loathe the other side as a prerequisite. While speaking at a rally in Pensacola in December 2017, days before the Alabama special senate election, and plugging for Roy Moore, the president made the incredible claim that we have a sick, rigged system.

> "It's being proven we have a rigged system. Doesn't happen so easy... This is a sick system from the inside. And there's no other country like our country, but we have a lot of sickness in some of our institutions," Trump told the crowd, adding, "There are powerful forces in Washington trying to sabotage our movement. These are bad people, very, very bad and evil people... But you know what, we're stopping them. You're seeing that right now."

But by labelling opponents as "very bad and evil people" and by attacking the system that he currently leads, Trump's actions seem eerily reminiscent of George Orwell's *1984*, where the Thought Police identified anyone who did not support or might compromise the Party's regime. Our system is not, however, and will never be, built around one person. Our judiciary, intelligence community, banking system, the media, and other institutions have served as the foundation of our country for over 200 years. We cannot let one man destroy them and if we passively accept that any criticism of the president is fake news, we are all co-conspirators.

LYCEUM ADDRESS

Many years before he became president, Abraham Lincoln gave a speech to the Young Men's Lyceum in Springfield, Illinois on January 27, 1838, titled *"The Perpetuation of Our Political Institutions."* Although portions of the speech were about the dangers of American slavery, the macro-lens of Lincoln's warning was that mobs or people who disrespected American institutions and courts could destroy the United States, including a single man. Put another way, the biggest threat to the United States would not come from without but from within. Below are excerpts of the future president's speech that we should diligently study today.

> *"Shall we expect some transatlantic military giant, to step the Ocean, and crush us at a blow? Never…At what point then is the approach of danger to be expected? I answer, if it ever reach us, it must spring up amongst us. It cannot come from abroad. If destruction be our lot, we must ourselves be its author and finisher."*

> *"Is it unreasonable then to expect, that some man possessed of the loftiest genius, coupled with ambition sufficient to push it to its utmost stretch, will at some time, spring up among us? And when such a one does, it will require the people to be united with each other, attached to the government and laws, and generally intelligent, to successfully frustrate his designs."*

> *"Let every American, every lover of liberty, every well-wisher to his posterity, swear by the blood of the Revolution, never to violate in the least particular, the laws of the country; and never to tolerate their violation by others…Passion has helped us; but can do so no more. It will in future be our enemy. Reason, cold, calculating, unimpassioned reason must furnish all the materials for our future support and defense. Let those materials be molded*

into general intelligence, sound morality, and in particular, a reverence for the constitution and laws." [10]

Lincoln understood that our nation is built upon the institutions that our forefathers built and that we must at all costs prevent destruction of those institutions from within. Our future will be insured not by passion but by cold, calculating reason, sound morality, and a reverence for the Constitution and laws. Lincoln presciently warned that a single man could rise up and that if he did, it would be necessary for people to unite to frustrate his designs.

People have not yet united in opposition and despite Trump's dismally approval ratings, his base consistently supports him through constant chaos and controversy. The one thing that confounds me more than anything else is this: why do Christians enthusiastically support Trump, the biggest purveyor of fake news ever?

GOD'S CHOSEN VESSEL?

It is obvious that Trump has tapped into something in the psyche of the American electorate. There is clearly an angst that exists in our country. However, as a Christian who believes that Jesus is my savior, I am perplexed at why Christians are blindly supporting Trump. Perhaps it's simply a belief that any Republican is better than any Democrat but that's not enough. Why do so many Christians refer to him as "God's anointed?"

After Trump criticized Mika Brzezinski of the TV show *"Morning Joe"* in July 2017, claiming that she had had a "bad face-lift," and after the release of a wrestling video showing him punching someone adorned with the CNN logo, Jerry Falwell, Jr., president of the Christian-based Liberty University in Lynchburg, Virginia, said the following during an interview on Fox News. *"We're finally getting back to a bold leader who's willing to speak his mind."* [11]

Criticizing a woman's looks is being bold? Punching a journalist is speaking one's mind? In what universe do Christians commend such behavior? Would Jesus approve?

In the aftermath of Charlottesville, many in the Evangelical Christian community condemned the neo-Nazis, Ku Klux Klan, and other white supremacists but very few criticized Trump directly. Falwell said Trump likely had more detailed information on protesters when he described "fine people" on both sides.

"One of the reasons I supported him is because he doesn't say what's politically correct, he says what is in his heart," Falwell told ABC's "This Week."[12]

On June 10, 2016, Trump spoke at a Christian evangelical conference. Ralph Reed, founder of the Christian Coalition and one of the organizers of the conference, enthusiastically supported Trump, saying the New Yorker has *"energized the evangelical vote in a way that past Republican candidates have failed to do."* He went on to say, *"We understand that perfection is not the measure that should be applied."*[13]

I accept that perfection should not be the measure because none of us is perfect, but then what is it exactly that has "energized" evangelicals? Is it his three marriages, or specifically, his leaving wives one and two for wives two and three? His prior support of abortion? His frequent cursing, even before the Boy Scouts, and including the F-bomb, in his public speeches? His statement that he has never asked God for forgiveness? His complete ignorance of the Bible (two Corinthians)? His refusal or inability to state his favorite Scripture verse? His comparing the Bible to "a great movie?" His comments to Howard Stern that he thinks he could have "nailed" Princess Diana and that he would loved to have "banged" Mariah Carey? His statement that if Ivanka was not his daughter that he would probably date her? His mocking a disabled reporter? His being the first owner of a casino with a strip club? His having filed bankruptcy four times? His statement that *"Part of the beauty of me is that I'm rich?"* His bragging about his wealth but being the first candidate in 50 years that has refused to produce his tax returns? His statement that he had raised $6 million for veterans when he hadn't?

His statement that acting presidential would be "boring as hell?" His telling Jimmy Fallon that he never apologizes because he is never wrong? His calling women dogs, pigs, and bitches? His comments about Megan Kelly having blood flow out of "wherever?" His tweeting of a glamourous photo of his wife next to a not so complimentary picture of Ted Cruz' wife that said, "*A picture's worth a thousand words?*" His comments that he supports torture, including waterboarding and "much more," even though it is illegal? His call to kill the families of enemy combatants? His calling for 1.2 billion people to be banned from entering the U.S.? His statement that Mexicans are rapists? His patting himself on the back about the Orlando attack about "being right" and suggesting that Obama was involved? His statements that he would "loosen" the libel laws and sue anyone who criticizes him? His threat against Amazon founder Jeff Bezos to use the anti-trust laws to harass him? His constant bragging, including about the size of his genitals? His comments that an American-born judge who has ruled against him was biased against him because his parents were born in Mexico? His refusal to disavow former KKK Grand Wizard David Duke? His statement that you have to be wealthy to be great?

His frequent statements with absolutely no basis to them, such as vaccinations cause autism, his suggestion that Ted Cruz' father was involved in the Kennedy assassination, and his witnessing "thousands and thousands" of Muslims cheering in New Jersey as the World Trade Center fell down? His revoking the press credentials of the *Washington Post* and nearly a dozen other media outlets during the campaign because they wrote things he didn't like? His release of a video after becoming president depicting him as a "Top Gun" fighter pilot shooting down a plane with the CNN logo?

His disrespectful and disparaging comments towards people who deserve respect, including senators, governors, foreign leaders, reporters, the Republican party? His comparing Ben Carson to a child molester and saying that he would sue John Kasich just "for fun?" His hundreds of insults to others about being weak, losers, pathetic, disgusting, disgraceful? His criticism of POW and war hero John McCain for being captured or Carly Fiorina's face? His blaming the falling of the World Trade Center on George W. Bush? His calling Senator Lindsey Graham a disgusting liar in August 2017 when Graham criticized him over Charlottesville? His angrily trashing the 2015 winner of *Time* Magazine's person of the year because it wasn't him? Is it his comments that if he didn't win the nomination that he would expect there to be riots? His statements that he would love to punch protesters in the face?

Was it his statement that when you're famous, you can grab women by the pussy? Telling more than 2000 lies in one year? Referring to certain immigrants as being from shit-hole countries? Since there has been so much pride, divisiveness and hate in both his campaign and his administration, why has Trump "energized" Evangelicals? How are Trump's actions and policies things that followers of Jesus can support? Why doesn't any of this bother Christians?

While Christians have been provided a conservative Supreme Court justice (although only after the Senate refused for nearly a year to allow a confirmation hearing for Merrick Garland), I believe the cost is too high. As Rod Dreher has written, "*Evangelicals have become loyal to a leader of shockingly low character. They have associated their faith with exclusion and bias. They have become another Washington interest group, striving for advantage rather than seeking the common good and a movement that should be known for grace is now known for its seething resentments.*"[14]

Even worse, Dreher refers to my fellow Christians as delusional. "*The idea that the robustly vulgar, combative, and morally comprised Trump will be an avatar for the restoration of Christian morality and social unity is beyond delusional. He is not a solution to America's cultural decline, but a symptom of it."* [15]

Many Christians have compared Trump to King David of Israel. Johnny Enlow, a Christian pastor from Atlanta, wrote in a New Years' Day message that Trump was like David. "*Though perhaps imperfectly, President Trump is as a David — specifically how David was as king. Whereas, Saul was a man of the people — David was a man chosen by God. God spoke to me, 'I chose Trump because I know some things that none of you know.'"* [16]

I believe the comparison falls short. After engaging in adultery and murder with Bathsheba and Uriah, the Lord sent the prophet Nathan to denounce David's actions. Where are the Nathans of today? Where are strong Christian leaders who have spoken up to say it's not alright for our elected leader to brag about grabbing women by their genitals and constantly lie? The silence of Christians has been overwhelming, but if we do nothing because we hope to get more conservative Supreme Court justices or policies on religious freedom that are to our liking, then there's a point where that strategy becomes a type of idolatry, because, as Dreher points out, it's merely "an attempt to manipulate the levers of history in favor of the causes we support."

Dreher's conclusion leaves no wiggle room and is breath-taking in its bluntness.

"He [Trump] has given no evidence of humility or dependence on others, let alone on God his Maker and Judge. He wantonly celebrates strongmen and takes every opportunity to humiliate and demean the vulnerable. He shows no curiosity or capacity to learn. He is, in short, the embodiment of what the Bible calls a fool." [17]

After the porn star and the Playmate came forward in early 2018 with their tawdry stories about the president, the Family Research Council said that its supporters give Trump a "mulligan" about his extramarital affairs.[18] "That was a long time ago," said Franklin Graham, one of Trump's staunchest supporters. "I'm more interested in who a person is today," ignoring the fact that Trump paid $130,000 to the porn star to keep her quiet weeks before the 2016 election. Robert Jeffress, the senior pastor at First Baptist Dallas, has said that he doesn't care if Trump is a religious phony but only that Trump has "embraced and enacted" policies favored by Evangelicals. But this position says there are no limits or boundaries "as long as we get what we want," which is not only is hypocritical, it's dangerous.

Harvey Weinstein was legitimately eviscerated, Matt Lauer justifiably lost his job and Al Franken was properly forced to resign from the senate as a result of their wrongful actions. The same is true across the country, in every industry. Outrageous conduct and words have consequences and prevent people from getting jobs and losing jobs every day in every city. But apparently that is not the case with the president as long as "we get what we want." But according to Peter Wehner, a senior fellow at the Ethics and Public Policy Center and former aide to Ronald Reagan and Bushes 41 and 43, when Evangelicals excuse the president's behavior and rhetoric, it's "complete hypocrisy" and has a "discrediting effect on faith."

Bill Clinton's conduct was wrong and he deserved impeachment. And if Trump's conduct is wrong, he deserves impeachment. Right is right and wrong is wrong and it doesn't change because of an R or a D. It's the height of hypocrisy to say to our kids that their wrongful conduct should be punished but that it's OK if the president does it because he gave us a Supreme Court Justice.

Everything in life has limits. Boundaries and restrictions exist. There is absolute truth. No one is above the law. You cannot support things that are right with conduct that is wrong. Lying is wrong, sexual harassment is wrong, abuse of power for personal enrichment is wrong, no matter how many things that you favor are dispensed in your direction.

For Christians who are concerned that the things they care about would suddenly be in jeopardy if Trump were gone, Hillary Clinton would not suddenly become president; Godly Mike Pence would. And so contorting oneself into a pretzel trying to excuse the inexcusable is, as Jesus would say, straining your water so you won't accidentally swallow a gnat but swallowing a camel instead. It's time to stop swallowing camels.

THE EMPEROR HAS NO CLOTHES

Danish author Hans Christian Anderson wrote a short story called *The Emperor's New Clothes* about two weavers who promised an emperor a new set of clothes that they said was invisible to anyone who is stupid or incompetent. When the emperor paraded around in his new clothes, no one dared to point out that the emperor was naked lest they be called stupid or incompetent. Finally, a child cried out, *"But he isn't wearing anything at all."*

I believe that Trump apologists, especially Christians, are making a huge mistake by refusing to point out that he's wearing no clothes. However, as in Anderson's story above, the emperor doesn't exist by himself. He doesn't operate in a vacuum for the emperor has subjects. And while we don't have subjects in our democracy, we have citizens whose consent is the prerequisite for governmental authority. If our government of over two centuries is being threatened by an assault on our institutions, that assault is only harmful if we allow it. We must not allow it. Christian and conservative support of this president is based on a premise that is, for lack of a better word, fake.

4

FRIENDS

─────────

"My dream is of a place and a time where America will once again be seen as the last best hope of earth."
Abraham Lincoln

"A good tree can't produce bad fruit and a bad tree can't produce good fruit. So every tree that does not produce good fruit is chopped down and thrown into the fire. Yes, just as you can identify a tree by its fruit, so you can identify people by their actions."
Jesus, Matthew 7:17-20

"When you go out into the world, watch out for traffic, hold hands, and stick together."
All I Really Need to Know I Learned in Kindergarten

During a game in 2016, early in the second quarter, Morgan Cox, the Baltimore Ravens' long-snapper, got hurt in a pileup on a Baltimore field-goal try. Cleveland defensive tackle Shaun Rogers and Baltimore guard Marshall Yanda fell on his left leg after he'd snapped the ball for the field goal and his knee concaved to the right. Cox screamed so loud, Rogers said later, that he knew he was hurt severely. Somehow, Cox limped to the sideline, where he collapsed and started rolling around in pain.

At first, the Ravens' doctors thought it was an MCL tear and that he could return to the game and gut it out. At halftime, upon further review, he was diagnosed with grade-three (severe) ACL and MCL tears. "But I knew I could get the job done," he said. "There's a lot of different ways of snapping. Some guys use their legs for power. I pretty much do it all with my arms. And I don't think it fully registered with me how serious it was. It was a big game, and I said, I'm fine to play. I went up to the guys on the line, and said, 'I'm gonna need some help. I'm gonna get the snap off, but you gotta help me after that' So when we went back out there, I heard Michael Oher say to the Browns, 'Stay off the snapper, stay off the snapper.'"

Cleveland's Rogers knew Cox was injured, having heard him scream in agony after the injury. On an extra point try, after the ball was over the line, Rogers saw Cox falling back awkwardly. He reached over and grabbed Cox's jersey to prevent him from falling and perhaps hurting the leg further.

"Unbelievable," Cox said. *"I felt this hand hold me up and just figured it was one of our guys, but it was Shaun Rogers. I'll never forget him for that."*

Football is a competitive sport and players constantly try to best each other, which means inflicting pain on each other. The other team, during the 60 minutes of play, is the enemy. Even so, the other players in the league are people, just like the ones on your team, and many become the best of friends. There is nothing improper about being a dedicated member of your team, whether it be the Chargers, the Patriots, or the

United States, and having friends on other teams, or from other countries. With our friends, we are stronger.

UNLOCKING OUR NATION'S FULL POWER

Throughout its history, the United States has developed and oscillated between two conflicting themes about foreign policy: 1) America serves its values best by perfecting democracy at home and acting as an example and beacon for the rest of the world, and 2) America's values impose on it an obligation to crusade for them around the world. Torn between these contradictory attitudes, as Henry Kissinger pointed out in his book *Diplomacy*, the U.S. has historically wavered between isolationism and interventionism.[1] Through its *America First* policy, the Trump Administration has made it clear that it intends to promote the former. There are two problems with this and children understand this better than adults.

Kids understand that if you focus just on yourself, you not only harm your friends by depriving them of your strengths and talents, you hurt yourself when you become isolated. As a result of this new, and still uncertain, policy, the U.S. has surrendered its global leadership role to China and Russia. This hurts the rest of the world and it harms each and every American.

Since the U.S. entered the world stage in 1917, its strength has been so dominant that the century's major international agreements, such as the United Nations Charter, have merely been rubber-stamped versions of American values and beliefs. But as former National Security Adviser Sandy Berger pointed out a few years ago, while the United States has never enjoyed greater power than it has had in the 21st century, it has rarely possessed so little influence. We can compel, he pointed out, but often cannot persuade.[2] This is even more true today.

Terrorism, and specifically ISIS, must be fought vigorously and America must maintain a strong military. However, the military must do more than fight wars and enemies; it must also, from time to time, be used for nation building and peace keeping. For most people of the world, localized armed conflict, poverty, disease, and environmental destruction are greater threats than ISIS. Towards this end, the United States must be seen as a peacemaker, helping to resolve disputes, helping to build the peacekeeping capabilities of other nations and willing to contribute money and troops when our interests and values are at stake.

In the coming years, we will have to rely more on persuasion than power to achieve our goals. We need allies to defeat our enemies, but we will need to combine our power with moral authority if we are to have a foreign and national security policy that is effective and fair. National security is more than the use of our brilliant military. It must also rely upon diplomacy, economic aid, financially responsible policies and respect for human rights. We cannot demand democracy for others if we fail to follow our own Constitution. We must be the world's great example of decency, democracy and human rights.

In 1948, Harry Truman said, "*If we wish to inspire the people of the world whose freedom is in jeopardy, if we wish to restore hope to those who have already lost their civil liberties, if we wish to fulfill the promise that is ours, we must correct the remaining imperfections in our practice of democracy.*"[3] As Peter Beinhart wrote in *The Good Fight*, expanding democracy at home "*wasn't just a matter of global public relations. It was the key to unlocking the nation's full power.*"[4] Truman understood that a superpower cannot always get its way just because of its power. "*We have to recognize – no matter how great our strength – that we must deny ourselves the license to always do as we please.*"[5]

We must fight our enemies vigorously, terrorists must be killed, and ISIS must be destroyed, but we must not just assume that we are morally superior; we must demonstrate it to the world. The greatest progress the U.S. ever made against global jihad, even greater than the killing of Osama bin Laden, was through the aid we gave after the 2005 tsunami, resulting in Indonesia becoming the first major Muslim country to support the U.S. war against terrorism.

It is incomplete, and intellectually lazy, to attribute all terrorism to "evil people." It is not a defense to the evil conduct of terrorists to seek to understand that jihadists often fill the vacuum that exists in failed and failing states by providing basic services. While some will no doubt argue that discussing the economic issues of terrorism is rationalizing, it is folly to bury our heads in the sand and ignore the reasons why people become terrorists in the first place. As easy as it is to explain that terrorists are evil and we are good, it's more complicated than that.

While we certainly need to carry out the military fight against terrorism and ISIS, we must also try, as Beinhart wrote, to reduce the extremely high female illiteracy rate in developing countries, push for economic reform, help others develop an independent judiciary, a free press, multiple political parties, and free elections. This will require monetary aid. While carrying out the Marshall Plan, the U.S. spent 15% of its budget on foreign aid. When Trump took office, it was less than one percent and he wants to dramatically reduce it even further.[6]

As Beinhart wrote, *national greatness is not inherited or declared; it is earned*. America should share power abroad because we recognize our limits and understand that such recognition is not a sign of weakness but of strength. Like Dirty Harry Callahan, played by Clint Eastwood, a nation "has got to know its limitations."

AMERICA FIRST

Under Donald Trump, the U.S. has given rebirth to a foreign policy first enunciated prior to World War II, which Trump has called "America

First." It is not clear if Trump truly understands the odious heritage of that doctrine and how it was implemented but the patriotic sounding "America First" has a controversial history.

> *"My foreign policy will always put the interests of the American people, and American security, above all else. That will be the foundation of every decision that I will make. America First will be the major and overriding theme of my administration,"* Trump said during the campaign, articulating a similar theme in his inauguration speech.

However, the slogan "America First" was also the name of the isolationist, defeatist, anti-Semitic national organization that urged the United States to appease Adolf Hitler. The America First Committee actually began at Yale University, where Gerald Ford, the future American president, and Potter Stewart, the future Supreme Court justice, along with others, drafted a petition stating, "*We demand that Congress refrain from war, even if England is on the verge of defeat.*"[7] Their solution was a negotiated peace with Hitler.

The growing organization soon had several hundred chapters and almost a million members. The first man to fly solo across the Atlantic, Charles Lindbergh, joined in April 1941 and became the committee's principal spokesman and chief drawing card at its rallies. America First struggled with the problem of the anti-Semitism of some of its leaders and many of its members and it is curious that this new change in American policy uses a term that reminds many of one of the ugliest chapters in recent American history.

LEAVING THE U.S. BEHIND

In practice, "America First" has meant downgrading decades-old alliances and long-held policies. Some allies already say they no longer look to the current White House for moral authority or leadership on the world stage. During his first official trip abroad, the president seemed at home with autocratic leaders such as Saudi Arabia's King Salman and Egypt's Abdel Fattah Sisi, while clashing with the Democratic leaders of European nations. Without mentioning Trump by name, the German Chancellor said at a campaign event that the era in which Europeans could "rely on others" is over.

However, more than any one policy, the downshift in U.S. influence is most worrying, according to experts. Quitting the Paris climate deal, which Trump did on June 1, 2017, will cede leadership to China. Decertifying the Iranian nuclear agreement, as Trump did in October 2017, angered our European allies and increased the chances of Iran getting a nuclear weapon. Overall, in his first year, Trump began to dismantle the American-centric global order that has existed for over 70 years through Democratic and Republican administrations. Because "America First" will sharply reduce the role the United States will play in the world, it will essentially result in "China First." It is clear that Trump sees monetary contributions to alliances as wasteful spending and views the long-standing American built system of institutions and trade as a series of "bad deals." It is no wonder that confidence in American leadership has fallen drastically in Trump's first year, having dipped 75% in Germany, 71% in South Korea, 70% in France, 57% in the UK and 54% in Japan.[8] This does not bode well for the remainder of Trump's term.

The President of the Council on Foreign Relations, Richard Haass, a State Department official during the George W. Bush Administration, told Anderson Cooper in January 2018 that the United States had "abdicated" its role as leader of the free world.

"The reason I use the word 'abdication' is what they've done is unilaterally — it wasn't forced on them... We've essentially decided in many cases that we simply don't think it's worth it, that we don't want to do it anymore," Haass stated, arguing that

it has made U.S. allies "less reliant on us, thinking more about how they have to carry out their own foreign policy and that it's diminished respect for us." [9]

What does this add up to? In a *Wall Street Journal* op-ed on May 31, 2017 by then National Security Adviser H.R. McMaster and Gary Cohn, then director of the National Economic Council, said "America First" means as follows:

"The president embarked on his first foreign trip with a clear-eyed outlook that the world is not a "global community" but an arena where nations, nongovernmental actors and businesses engage and compete for advantage. We bring to this forum unmatched military, political, economic, cultural, and moral strength. Rather than deny this elemental nature of international affairs, we embrace it. At every stop in our journey, we delivered a clear message to our friends and partners: Where our interests align, we are open to working together to solve problems and explore opportunities." [10]

In Trump's view, nations share only a thirst for power and wealth and nothing else. The idea of shared values and a shared fate apparently don't matter. The world is simply a transactional zero-sum game where some win and some lose, but power is not a commodity that governments can store and control. Since the end of World War II, we have lived in a global community, in accordance with an accepted international order, and there are limits to what a country can do to protect its citizens through isolationism. Global issues such as climate change, terrorists and disease don't care about fancy sounding doctrines, nor are they stopped by walls or threats from the White House. Trump's erroneous worldview ignores real dangers and, consequently, Americans are less safe.

Past American presidents have believed that alliances would create increased wealth and security which would, in turn, benefit both the

United States and its allies. But since "America First" is based on cutthroat competition and suspicion, it is hard to see how this will extend American security and prosperity.

AMERICA LAST?

Not since the Berlin wall came down has a U.S. president pursued such a go-it-alone strategy in international affairs. While Trump's first overseas trip left bruised feelings in Europe, it was his action on climate change that will likely create ripple effects around the globe for years to come. Since previous U.S. administrations negotiated the Paris accord, the withdrawal will impact America's ability to enter into other international agreements in the future.

John Kerry, who helped negotiate the Paris deal, said that Trump mischaracterized what the accord required, what it would achieve and who would benefit from it. "*This step does not make America first,*" Kerry told CBS Evening News. "*It makes America last.*"[11]

Numerous G20 leaders were not shy about voicing their disappointment with Trump's withdrawal decision. In a joint statement, the 28 nations in the EU and China said they remained committed to full implementation of the Paris accord. Just before the G-20 summit, Japan and the European Union announced a trade deal that illustrates how the "America First" approach to trade and policy isn't working. By creating a mammoth-free trade area, it is anticipated that the deal will greatly expand global trade and lower barriers to the exporting of cars between Japan and Europe. While a trade victory for both parties, it was a clear snub to the U.S.

On a host of other issues, Trump has also irritated our allies. Forging ahead with his campaign promises, he's shown disdain for the North American Free Trade Agreement (NAFTA) and abruptly pulled out of the 12 nation Trans-Pacific Partnership (TPP). Regarding steel, Trump frequently criticized suppliers for cheating on steel prices and threatened tariffs against many countries, before actually imposing them in March 2018. Trump's move to block entry into the U.S. of people from predominantly Muslim countries drew condemnation from many G20 leaders. Trump also doubled down on his promise to build a Mexican border wall, although Mexico is not paying for it and the $1.3 trillion budget he signed in March 2018 allocated only $1.6 billion instead of the $25 billion he was seeking.

On September 19, 2017, President Trump took to the floor of the United Nations General Assembly for the first time. Ignoring climate change, he said that certain parts of the world are "in fact, going to hell," he attacked "loser terrorists," he declared the Iran nuclear deal all but dead and an "embarrassment," and revived his use of "radical Islamic terrorism." He then proceeded to the main part of the show: North Korea, where he stunned many in the Hall with unprecedented bluntness and greatly escalated already high tensions.

> *"The United States has great strength and patience, but if it is forced to defend itself or its allies, we will have no choice but to totally destroy North Korea."*

When Harry Truman addressed the United Nations in 1945, he encouraged countries to park their self-interests for the greater good of mankind.

> *"We all have to recognize — no matter how great our strength — that we must deny ourselves the license to do always as we please. If any nation would keep security for itself, it must be ready and willing to share security with all. That is the price which each nation will have to pay for world peace."* [12]

Trump apparently did not see the irony that Kim Jong Un, Iran's Ayatollah Ali Khameni, Syria's Assad, Venezuela's Maduro and other dictators that he harshly criticized are all pursuing the same kind of "me first" policy that he promotes. Rather than their minds and policies being changed to come more in line with the international community, they no doubt left New York convinced that they are right to do so.

In March 2018, shortly after China's Xi Jinping was able to abolish term limits so that he could stay in power for life, Trump told a group of donors at a fundraiser at Mar-a-Lago, "*He was able to do that. I think that's great. Maybe we'll have to give that a shot someday.*" The audience laughed and the White House later said that he was joking but there is no doubt that Trump admires dictators. Regarding Vladimir Putin, "He's getting an 'A'," Trump once said and is "very much a leader." Turkey's Erdogan, who has also been laying the groundwork for a dictatorship is "getting very high marks" even as human rights and democracy monitoring organizations have raised concerns about his attacks on free speech and democracy. After Philippines president Rodrigo Duerte unleashed a brutal war on suspected drug traffickers that caused more than 12,000 deaths, Trump praised him for doing "an unbelievable job on the drug problem." Contrasted with the frequent praise he heaps upon dictators and tyrants, Trump constantly criticizes democratically elected leaders from some of our strongest allies. Like dictators, Trump hates the media and like many tyrants, he wants to use the judicial system to punish and crush his political opponents. But the U.S. is based on certain ideals like democracy and freedom and such conduct is un-American.

AMERICA AGAINST THE WORLD

President Trump formally recognized Jerusalem as the capital of Israel in December of 2017 and announced that the United States would move its embassy there from Tel Aviv, reversing almost 70 years of American foreign policy. Trump promised to move the embassy during the presidential campaign, a position that appealed to Evangelical voters and pro-Israel American Jews and the announcement was a hit with that bloc.

However, it was harshly criticized by just about everyone else, alienated much of the world, and sparked violent protests.

Jerusalem's status is fiercely contested, with each side disputing the other's claims. Palestinians view East Jerusalem as the capital of a future Palestinian state, and most of the world considers it occupied territory. For decades, the United States has attempted to mediate peace by serving as an honest broker. That will be much more difficult to accomplish since the U.S. has essentially taken sides. Since Trump's campaign first started, he had made it clear that he is anti-Muslim and he has repeatedly acted in a way to reinforce that belief.

On December 21, 2017, the United Nations soundly condemned the decision, including almost all of America's major allies, except Israel. U.N. Ambassador Nikki Haley tweeted that the U.S. "would take names" and gave a speech seeped in personal resentment and victimology, blasting the nations of the world for having the audacity to criticize America.

"America will put our embassy in Jerusalem. That is what the American people want us to do, and it is the right thing to do. No vote in the United Nations will make any difference on that, but this vote will make a difference on how Americans look at the UN and on how we look at countries who disrespect us in the UN. And this vote will be remembered."[13]

Just prior to Trump's announcement on Jerusalem, in late November 2017, Trump retweeted three videos from the deputy leader of Britain First: a far-right, ultranationalist, neo-fascist hate group that organizes "Christian patrols" and "invades" mosques trying to intimidate those who attend religious services. The videos painted Muslims as anti-Christian criminals. Although the videos were full of inaccuracies and errors (the supposed Muslim foreigner beating up a European on crutches was, in fact, not a foreigner and was prosecuted), they were clearly aimed at demonizing Muslims. Aside from the indecency of the retweets and the complete ignoring of the First Amendment guarantee of religious freedom, Trump's actions also damaged American security. When the United States vilifies Muslims, it damages our relationships with Muslim-majority nations whose help we need. It also inflicts serious damage to America's power in the world by alienating allies, including Great Britain, our closest ally.

> *"British people overwhelmingly reject the prejudiced rhetoric of the far right, which is the antithesis of the values that this country represents – decency, tolerance and respect,"* British Prime Minister Theresa May said. *"It is wrong for the president to have done this."*[14]

Although Trump's actions were nearly universally criticized, they were praised by David Duke. *"Trump retweets video of crippled white kid in Europe being beaten by migrants, and white people being thrown off a roof and then beaten to death. He's condemned for showing us what the fake news media WON'T. Thank God for Trump! That's why we love him!"* [15]

What made this juvenile and malicious action even worse is that White House press secretary Sarah Huckabee Sanders said it didn't matter whether the inflammatory videos are real or not, because "the threat is real." Think about that. The truth does not matter, the White House said, conjuring up once again images of Orwell's *1984*.

Sure, the world is dangerous. Absolutely, we need to have a strong military. No doubt, we have to pursue our best interests. I was an army officer, was stationed in Europe, served with the Green Berets and volunteered for the Persian Gulf War. I know that there is evil and that there are bad people. Yes, the United States must pursue its best interests, but that doesn't mean we need to alienate everyone else. There are over 200 countries and international affairs are not just zero-sum relationships where "if I win, you must lose." The world is not always transactional. When we invaded Iraq in 2003 with our overwhelming power and "shock and awe," we did not need allies. But we sure could have used them down the road.

Life is hard, but is much easier with friends. Ask any kid.

5

DARKNESS

"*Character is like a tree and reputation like a shadow. The shadow is what we think of it; the tree is the real thing.*"
Abraham Lincoln

"*I am the light of the world. If you follow me, you won't have to walk in darkness because you will have the light that leads to life.*"
Jesus, John 8:12

"*Don't take things that aren't yours.*"
All I Really Need to Know I Learned in Kindergarten

The official rules of the National Football League require footballs to be inflated to a gauge pressure between 12.5 and 13.5 pounds per square inch (psi). A deliberately under-inflated football may be easier to grip, throw and catch, or inhibit fumbling, especially in cold rainy conditions. The 2014 AFC Championship Game was played at Gillette Stadium, home of the New England Patriots, who hosted the Indianapolis Colts. During the first half, Patriots quarterback Tom Brady threw an interception. After the interception, a Colts equipment manager measured the pressure of the ball on the sideline and the team notified the NFL that they *"understood that there was a problem with the inflation level of a Patriots football."*[1]

The Patriots won 45–7 and the NFL began an investigation to "get to the bottom of Deflategate." The investigation concluded that it was "more probable than not" that New England Patriots equipment personnel were deliberately circumventing the rules. Further, it was determined as being more probable than not that Brady was "generally aware" of the deflation. The NFL suspended Brady without pay for four games, based on "substantial and credible evidence" that Brady knew Patriots employees were deflating footballs and that he failed to cooperate with investigators. The Patriots were also fined $1 million and had to forfeit their first round pick in the 2016 NFL draft as well as their fourth round pick in the 2017 NFL draft.

The NFL Players Association (NFLPA) filed an appeal but NFL Commissioner Roger Goodell upheld the suspension, citing Brady's destruction of his cell phone as a critical factor. Investigators had requested access to nearly 10,000 text messages, none of which were able to be retrieved. The NFLPA filed for an injunction in federal court and the judge threw out Brady's suspension, although the U.S. Court of Appeals later reinstated it. Tom Brady sat out the first four games of the 2016 season, but then led the Patriots to the Super Bowl a few months later.

"Deflategate" grabbed a lot of press. Some thought Brady and the Patriots committed criminal acts while many thought it was a lot to do about nothing, but there is no doubt that the star quarterback and the Patriots made it difficult to discover what had happened. There was little transparency and where investigators sought light they found only darkness.

OFFICERS, DIRECTORS, AND SHAREHOLDERS

Government is supposed to work in the sunlight so that all the citizens can see what is going on. It is supposed to be transparent. The public has a right to know what our officials are saying and doing as does posterity. The United States is like a large corporation. We have neither the time nor the knowledge to get involved in all the nuts and bolts of running a nation of 300 million people and so we elect people to represent us. We are like shareholders. We own the company and are entitled to see how the officers are running things.

We also have a media that is supposed to keep our elected officials honest and to hold them accountable for their actions. Admittedly, the media sometimes goes too far, sometimes makes mistakes and is sometimes biased. Overall, the media serves a vital function in keeping its pulse on the heartbeat of America.

The Trump Administration is the least transparent in U.S. history. Trump has held very few press conferences, he has refused to release his tax returns, he has waffled on responding to numerous lawsuits claiming that he is wrongly mixing his businesses with the government, and his communications team has slowly been curtailing the media's access to the administration.

In October 2017, after it was reported that Secretary of State Rex Tillerson had called Trump a "moron," something Tillerson never denied, Trump tweeted as follows: "*With all the Fake News coming out of NBC and Networks, at what point is it appropriate to challenge their license? Bad for country!*" Trump then doubled down by later tweeting: "*Network news has become so partisan, distorted and fake that licenses must be challenged and, if appropriate, revoked. Not fair to public!*"

In other words, the president of the United States was suggesting that the Federal Communications Commission should punish news outlets that criticize him. Besides the fact that the licenses are not held by the networks, it was stunning to see a U.S. president work so hard to silence the media and keep the public in the dark.

Is this administration doing its best to look out for the interests of each shareholder? What steps are being taken to spread light on the decisions of the White House? After all, the government derives its powers from the consent of the governed. If we are not kept in the loop, if the public is kept in the dark, then the government's power and authority evaporates. In a January 2018 tweet, Trump misquoted conservative columnist Michael Goodwin: "*His* [Trump] *is turning out to be an enormously* _consensual_ *presidency*," instead of the actual word, "consequential." While I would not agree that his is a consequential presidency so far, it most certainly isn't a consensual one since the public has been totally left in the dark.

ENRICHMENT

In 2017, Trump spent an astonishing 110 days at one of his properties. While all presidents are entitled to vacations, Trump's frequent visits enrich his pockets and smack of hypocrisy. Trump routinely bashed Obama for golfing and said he would never have time for golf because he would be so busy. "*I just want to stay in the White House and work my ass off*," he said during the campaign, but he spent an incredible 86 days at one of his golf clubs in 2017.

While most presidents have maintained and visited their personal homes while in office, Trump's situation is different because his residences are part of his business empire. So, when the Department of Homeland Security spends taxpayer money to move and protect the president around his own properties, some of it spills into Trump Organization coffers. Asking how much money the Trump-led government is spending on businesses that he owns and tallying up government spending involved in his many weekend trips to his resorts is a legitimate question.

The answer and the ramifications remain to be seen.

The Trump Organization leased the 263-room Trump International Hotel in Washington from the General Services Administration in 2013 and pays the federal agency $250,000 in rent each month. In a sense, Trump is both the landlord and the tenant and gets richer every month because of this unprecedented arrangement. One of Washington's most expensive hotels, it brought in $19.7 million between its opening in the fall of 2016 and mid-April 2017, according to Trump's financial disclosures,[2] lending fuel to the argument that anyone seeking favor from the White House has an incentive to stay there. Each month, the average rate per room goes up, as have membership fees at his various country clubs.

In June of 2017, the hotel's management admitted to the *Washington Post* that it wanted to capitalize on the president's popularity and therefore markets the hotel to Republican groups that embrace Trump's politics. For Trump supporters, the hotel has become a frequent stop for Republican lobbyists, conservative groups, and foreign entities. Trump himself has showcased the hotel as the destination for GOP loyalists. In July of 2017, about 300 Republican donors, paying $35,000 apiece, gathered for a fundraiser and an estimated $10 million was raised for Trump's campaign, the Republican National Committee and other GOP groups, according to news reports at the time.[3] The hotel has also hosted events for many Republican members of Congress, according to campaign spending disclosures.

Although Trump has turned over the hotel's management to his two eldest sons, he has retained his ownership interest and will eventually reap the profits. Furthermore, since only people who support Trump are welcome, he is getting richer from like-minded people who may want something in return. As a result, Trump is financially motivated to listen to, and govern on behalf of, only a portion of the electorate.

All in all, 64 trade groups, foreign governments, and Republican candidates stayed at or held events at Trump properties in 2017 including approximately three dozen at the Trump International Hotel,[4] while the Defense Department employees spent over $138,000 at Trump properties in the first eight months of the new administration.[5] In just the first two months of 2018 alone, the Republican National Committee spent more than $424,000.00 at properties owned by the president, more than 100 times more than was spent during the same time in 2017, and is on track to spend upwards of $2.5 million at Trump properties in 2018 and possibly tens of millions over the course of the Trump presidency.[6] Moreover, the RNC spends more than $35,000.00 a month to rent office space at Trump Tower in New York City, which is used by the Trump reelection campaign.[7]

According to an investigation by *USA TODAY* in September 2017, dozens of lobbyists and contractors who make their living influencing the government pay President Trump's companies for membership in his private golf clubs. Members of Trump's clubs, who pay initiation fees that can exceed $100,000, plus thousands more in annual dues, included at least 50 executives whose companies hold federal contracts and 21 lobbyists and trade group officials.[8] For the first time in U.S. history, wealthy people with interests before the government have a chance for close access to the president through payments that personally enrich him. Walter Schaub, the former Office of Government Ethics ("OGE") director, said even conversations that have nothing to do with the government can raise ethics concerns. The Washington lobbying and contracting worlds are built on access, Schaub points out, and that makes any opportunity to meet the president valuable. The very people Trump is hanging out with *"are paying to be there in that setting with him,"* said Barbara Perry, director of presidential studies at the University of Virginia's Miller Center. *"This is unprecedented on so many levels."*[9]

In March 2018, ProPublica reported that the Trump Organization ordered 12-inch replicas of the presidential seal to be used as tee markers at Trump golf courses.[10] Under federal law, the seal's use is permitted only for official government business and while Trump supporters will no doubt shrug their shoulders, marking the tee at a Trump golf club most certainly does not meet that standard.

Moreover, Trump projects are taking place all over the world. The Indonesia government is planning to build a road to shorten the drive between the airport and the new Trump resort and golf course. The Panamanian government took steps to ensure that a sewer system around the Trump skyscraper would be completed. Other foreign governments have donated public land for Trump projects, in addition to granting permits and easing up on environmental regulations.[11] Since Trump never divested himself from his businesses, he is clearly profiting by being president. Since he refuses to release his tax returns, there is no way to know whether his decisions as president are being influenced by a profit motive.

If you would like to snag a Trump "Classic Stripe Tech Polo" shirt, you can order one from Trumpstore.com for only $105.00.[12] This site, not to be confused with DonaldJTrump.com, the profits from which flow to the Trump campaign, sells all the Trump stuff you would ever need, including a Trump baseball cap for just $35.00, and all the profits go to the president himself. Is this legal? Although most federal employees would be barred from profiting off their positions because of conflict of interest rules, the rules don't apply to the president.

Many Trump supporters are downplaying it, but there is no doubt that the president and his family are being personally enriched through this presidency in an unprecedented fashion.

In July of 2017, Schaub resigned, frustrated that the White House was making a mockery of ethical guidelines that have been followed by previous administrations. Schaub has called for major changes in federal law, saying in an interview in July of 2017 that the Trump Administration had flouted long-accepted norms in a way that threatened to undermine the United States' ethical standards, which have been admired around the world.

"It's hard for the United States to pursue international anti-corruption and ethics initiatives when we're not even keeping our own side of the street clean. It affects our credibility," Schaub said on the same weekend that Trump tweeted seven times that he would be spending it at one of his golf clubs that was being paid to host the U.S. Women's Open golf tournament. *"I think we are pretty close to a laughingstock at this point,"* Schaub added.[13]

At the beginning of the new Administration, some government agencies were ordered to change or drop web pages and even stop using social medial channels, raising red flags. Since Trump repeatedly and vigorously claimed that Obama was hiding something, his unwillingness to be totally transparent can only suggest that he must be hiding something.

"NOTHING TO LEARN"

On the campaign trail, Trump was an enthusiastic advocate for accountability and disclosure. Where were Hillary Clinton's speeches behind closed doors to Wall Street financiers, he asked? Why had she used private email servers instead of ones maintained by the government? What had Clinton done as secretary of state for her foundation's donors? However, once elected, Trump has absolutely refused to embrace transparency for his own administration.

The *New York Times* reported in October that the real estate mogul had written off a loss of nearly *$1 billion* on his 1995 tax returns, allowing him to potentially avoid paying federal income taxes for 18 years. The public is entitled to know, however, if the president has earned as much as he's claimed, if he's paid any taxes at all, if he's given any money to charity as he has bragged about and how steeped in Russia he really is.

The tax return issue crystallizes the entire transparency issue. Trump previously told the *Associated Press* that there was "nothing to learn from them" and that he didn't think voters cared. However, voters should be given the information they need to make educated decisions and not be asked to vote on faith alone. "Believe me" is not enough. Although Republicans in Congress keep voting to protect Trump's returns from being released, as the shareholders in the corporation, you and I should be entitled to see anything that sheds light on the person we made the most powerful in the world, especially since the tax cut of December 22, 2017 will reportedly enrich him and his family to the tune of more than *one billion* dollars.

The billionaire president, who has been under constant fire from Democrats, but not Republicans, for blurring the line between his personal financial affairs and his official duties, signed into law in December 2017 the most sweeping changes to the nation's tax policy in 30 years and no one knows for sure how it will affect him personally, although the overwhelming consensus is that the tax bill will enrich him immensely. Trump has repeatedly insisted that he would have higher taxes if the tax bill passed. It would not be good for him, he repeatedly said. *"Believe me."* Since nearly every expert has said clearly that he and his family will benefit enormously from this bill, he is lying.

Why doesn't this bother Republicans?

In February 2016, Trump claimed several times that he would release his returns in the future. Eventually, Trump started saying that he couldn't release his returns because they were under audit, a claim first made during a presidential primary debate. During his first news conference as president-elect, Trump was asked about releasing his returns. *"The only ones that care about my tax returns are the reporters, okay?"* Trump said. Asked if he didn't that think the public cared, Trump said: *"I don't think so. I won. I mean, I became president. No, I don't think they care at all."*

People do care, however, and polls consistently show that they expect him to release his returns. Just days after the Inauguration, over 500,000 people petitioned for his returns to be released through the White House's "We the People" web site and by September, over 1,000,000 had signed the petition. In December 2017, the White House "temporarily" shut down the site,[14] emboldened, no doubt, by repeated loyalty from Congressional Republicans who have consistently defeated Democratic efforts to force the president to release his tax returns.

USA, INC.

In the book *America's Promise Restored: Preventing Culture, Crusade and Partisanship from Wrecking Our Nation*, Harlan Ullman suggested that our government leaders be held to the same standards and requirements of Sarbanes-Oxley as are corporate leaders.[14] Under Sarbanes-Oxley, for example, CEOs must verify that the information contained in balance sheets and the like not contain any untrue statement. No one doubts, Ullman says, that visibility, accuracy, reliability, and truthfulness, the reasons for Sarbanes-Oxley's implementation, are not less important for the government than they are for the private sector. Why not, therefore, increase accountability for our leaders by requiring them to verify budgets and fiscal requests and reports?

Whatever argument has existed in the past for transparency, the issues with Donald Trump, the current CEO of USA, Inc., have been magnified a hundred-fold. His presidency has a tremendous impact on his vast business empire and how the two interact affects every shareholder. We have a right to know what the CEO and the board are doing. Truth and light offers the only right way for the government to obtain the consent of the governed.

Why, with all the problems we are facing, have I chosen transparency as an urgent issue for our nation? I wouldn't have given it the same level of importance two years ago but we are moving down a path where our government is operating in the dark more and more. History has shown that authoritarian leaders, who Trump respects and emulates, care very little about keeping their citizens involved. People need to know what's going on with their president and their government. "Trust me," he says. "Believe me," he says. That's not enough. We are shareholders in this business and have a right to know what is going on. Unfortunately, our board of directors (Congress) apparently believe the CEO can do whatever he wants and be personally enriched at the same time. There is no possible justification for this other than political.

Multiple lawsuits were filed in 2017 regarding the alleged violation by the president of the Constitution's Emoluments Clause, the clause that is supposed to prevent foreign governments from trying to exert undue influence over our officials. In other words, it was designed to ensure that government officials serve the American people and not themselves. The legal problem in each of these cases is "standing." A plaintiff in a civil lawsuit has to allege an injury of some sort. If Trump's actions allow him to enrich himself, how is any specific person injured? Numerous experts believed that this issue would doom the existing cases, leaving only one course of action: action by Congress. Unfortunately, Congress has remained a "potted plant" on this matter and nothing is likely to be done with Republicans in control.

However, on March 28, 2018, a federal court judge ruled that the attorneys general of Maryland and the District of Columbia could proceed with their case against the president. The plaintiffs had alleged that Trump properties were putting other hotels at a competitive disadvantage, although the judge limited the case to involve only the Trump International Hotel in D.C. The judge found the arguments that only Congress can address this issue "particularly concerning" because Congress can be controlled by one party and choose to do nothing.[15]

While this issue has not received as much attention as the Mueller probe or Stormy Daniels, this case could ultimately have a significant impact.

If Democrats regain control of Congress in November 2018, impeachment proceedings will probably be quickly initiated and most Democrats will vote for impeachment while most Republicans will be against. The likely outcome will be that Trump will not be removed, everything will be repeated a few years down the road against a Democratic president and our political system will become even more broken and tribalized.

The only solution at this point is for Republicans to speak up and demand changes. I am not holding my breath but since this broken system will hurt my children, I will not give up hope.

CIRCLE OF TRUST

For four years, I attended the University of Florida and remain a proud member of the "Gator Nation." I have especially loved the three football national championships the Gators won in 1996, 2006, and 2008. For three seasons, Coach Urban Meyer enabled and pandered to his elite players, what the players called Meyer's "Circle of Trust." In the 2008 season opener, Meyer said a few elite players would miss the game with injuries. According to multiple sources, however, those players had failed drug tests and were sitting out as part of standard university punishment.[16] By publicly stating that they were injured, rather than admitting that they were being disciplined, Meyer was creating a divide between the haves and have-nots on the team.

Trump has developed his own "Circle of Trust," where the rules do not apply to him and his family. But government cannot function if there is no trust, democracy does not work in the dark and true freedom is impossible if a nation's leader and his small circle of family and advisors financially profit from the presidency.

PART TWO

THE LONG SEASON

DEFENSE

6

HEALTH

"Be sure you put your feet in the right place, then stand firm."
Abraham Lincoln

"Healthy people don't need a doctor-sick people do."
Jesus, Matthew 9:12

"Warm cookies and cold milk are good for you."
All I Really Need to Know I Learned in Kindergarten.

NFL players' thoughts about career-ending injuries lurk in the back of their minds every time they take the field and a recent study published in the *American Journal of Sports Medicine* shows that tendon and ligament injuries are potentially worse than broken and dislocated bones when it comes to complete recovery. Researchers found that tears of the ACL and injured tendons in the kneecap and the Achilles heel were more likely to keep players off the field. The study analyzed 559 NFL players who underwent procedures to repair a variety of orthopedic injuries from 2003 to 2013. Those treated for ACL tears and kneecap tendon injuries were most likely to suffer sustained declines in their level of performance.

There is no doubt that every player in the NFL receives the best healthcare possible. Is the same true for the other 300 million plus Americans who do not play professional football? No. Can you imagine a team that only treats certain players while abandoning the rest of the team to fend for themselves? That is how our healthcare system has worked in recent decades. We have the highest quality of care in the world for those with money. For those without it, forget it. If you are in the vast middle, your care has been determined by the vagaries of your employer. Maybe you had good care and maybe you didn't.

For the last several years, we have heard countless statements promoting the *Affordable Care Act* ("ACA"), also known as Obamacare, and even more attacks on it as responsible for all the evil in the world. Most are insured through their employer and are not affected by either Obamacare or any replacement. Whether you are insured through your employer or through Obamacare, the American healthcare system has numerous flaws that need to be reformed.

For over 50 years, healthcare spending exceeded the increase in national income by more than 2.5% per year.[1] In 1965, federal expenditures for health were less than half of one percent of gross domestic product. By 2004, such expenditures had increased by more than 1000% to about one-sixth of the total economy.[2] Those with insurance sought every possible service available, no matter the cost, while almost 50 million Americans had no health insurance at all.

The United States pays more for its healthcare, both on a per capita and an absolute basis, than any country in the world. The reasons include high administrative costs, doctors' salaries, hospital stays and the prevalence of specialists, among others. The biggest reason is the increase of tests and the utilization of expensive technology. As one person receives an expensive and perhaps unnecessary procedure, somebody else might be denied basic treatment. And so, the moral issue becomes whether it is fair to limit or deny basic treatment to some people while financing questionable and expensive procedures to others. Moreover, many Americans who have poor or no insurance coverage subsidize those with good coverage directly through payroll taxes or indirectly through massive tax subsidies.

How should we finance state of the art care that helps patients only a little bit, if at all? The logical answer would be to let the doctors decide, but they make more money when expensive procedures are used. The way to generate the largest bills is to buy expensive technologies like MRIs and CAT scanners, the costs of which are written off when large numbers of people use them. Nowhere else is this possible, since in no other industry are the buyer and the seller of a service in effect the same person. Another factor behind rising healthcare costs is that of defensive medicine designed to minimize malpractice lawsuits.

The consequences will be catastrophic unless there are some significant changes. Per capita healthcare spending in the U.S. exceeds every nation in the world by a large amount with no discernible increased level of care. If the trend continues, by 2051, annual increases in total healthcare spending will absorb all of the nation's economic growth.[3] The situation will get worse every year and if we do not act, our children and grandchildren will suffer the consequences. Blaming the other political party is not enough.

A RIGHT FOR ALL OR A PRIVILEGE FOR FEW?

Is healthcare a right for all or is it above a certain basic level the equivalent of a commodity which should be, in part, rationed by price? Prior to the enactment of Obamacare, approximately 45 million people had no insurance, about 1/6 of the population. However, that does not mean that they did not receive healthcare. They often did, in the form of emergency care. Hospitals that handle a large number of uninsured ER patients can lose hundreds of millions of dollars per year. These losses have to be absorbed somehow and are usually shifted to paying patients and are further absorbed in the form of higher Medicare costs.

Moreover, thousands of uninsured Americans die each year because of having no healthcare coverage. Bringing millions of Americans into the mainstream of the healthcare system is both good ethics and sound policy, but the uninsured have always lacked political clout and have been comprised of by, in large part, younger Americans, recent immigrants and laid off workers in their fifties and sixties. They have always been too politically weak to have any impact unless they can join forces with the insured.

There are few things more complicated than healthcare but we must first answer the threshold question: Is healthcare a right for everyone or is it not? Former Vice-President Joe Biden said, "*If Republican leadership wants to improve the ACA, let's first come to an agreement that everyone should have health coverage. Then, based on that premise, let's have a debate about how best to improve care and reduce costs. Let's again make the commitment that in America, healthcare is a right for all, not a privilege for the wealthy.*"[4]

Not everyone agrees.

OBAMACARE, REPEAL AND REPLACE

The *Affordable Care Act* was enacted in 2010. It instantly became a lightning rod and on over 50 occasions, the Republicans in Congress attempted without success to repeal it. When Donald Trump became President, the Republicans made repeal and replace their top legislative item. Trump had boasted that he would quickly and easily replace Obamacare with an alternative that everyone would love. "*You're going to have such great healthcare at a tiny fraction of the cost,*" he claimed. "*It's going to be so easy."* When it came to the House for a vote in March of 2017, Speaker Paul Ryan pulled it when it became apparent that it did not have the votes. Some modifications were made, however, and six weeks later, the *American Healthcare Act* ("AHCA") was passed by the House without debate or hearings, without support from hospitals and medical organizations and most importantly, without a score from the non-partisan Congressional Budget Office. A short time later, the CBO announced that over 23 million people would lose coverage. Bad news, of course, but House members seemed to say, "Well, it's up to the Senate now to fix it. We did our part."

Despite Trump's earlier declaration of victory, he later told Senators that the House bill was "mean." The House version was dead on arrival. For weeks, a committee of 13 men worked in secret on a bill that was only released to the remainder of the Senate and the public days before the scheduled vote. Within 24-48 hours, however, vocal and strong opposition had emerged. Majority Leader McConnell then scheduled a vote on a procedural motion to see if there were votes to continue debate and barely eked out a 51-50 vote on July 25, 2017, the tie being broken by Vice-President Pence. Senator McCain, who had just undergone surgery, was flown back for the vote and, with stiches on his face, gave a dramatic speech. His speech acknowledged the fact that tribalism was preventing success.

> *"Our deliberations today – not just our debates, but the exercise of all our responsibilities: authorizing government policies, appropriating the funds to implement them, exercising our advice, and consent role – are often lively and interesting. They can be sincere and principled, but they are more partisan, more tribal more of the time than any other time I remember. Our deliberations can still be important and useful, but I think we'd all agree they haven't been overburdened by greatness lately. And right now, they aren't producing much for the American people.*

"Both sides have let this happen. Let's leave the history of who shot first to the historians. I suspect they'll find we all conspired in our decline — either by deliberate actions or neglect. We've all played some role in it. Certainly, I have. Sometimes, I've let my passion rule my reason. Sometimes, I made it harder to find common ground because of something harsh I said to a colleague. Sometimes, I wanted to win more for the sake of winning than to achieve a contested policy." [5]

Acknowledging that they weren't getting much done, McCain made the crazy suggestion that perhaps the two parties should work together.

"What have we to lose by trying to work together to find those solutions? We're not getting much done apart. I don't think any of us feels very proud of our incapacity. Merely preventing your political opponents from doing what they want isn't the most inspiring work. There's greater satisfaction in respecting our differences, but not letting them prevent agreements that don't require abandonment of core principles, agreements made in good faith that help improve lives and protect the American people." [6]

Will the two parties forgo political posturing and work together or will they continue in their tribal pronouncements and mean-spirited attacks? That remains to be seen.

After several failures, the Senate tried in one last effort to pass a limited repeal of Obamacare, but the "skinny repeal" bill failed in the wee hours of July 28, 2017 after Sen. McCain sealed the fate of the GOP repeal push with a dramatic thumbs-down. Suddenly, the plan, seven years in the making, to repeal Obamacare, which was going to be "so easy," was relegated to the ash heap of history.

"I'M NOT GOING TO OWN IT"

Although he had never made any attempt to convince people of why they should support the repeal efforts, Trump continued his vow after the failure of the skinny bill to sabotage the *Affordable Care Act*. "*Let Obamacare implode, then deal,*" Trump said. Although it's not clear exactly what Trump wanted, it is clear is that he intended to do everything possible to sabotage the ACA out of anger and spite. Many Republicans had genuine principled reasons for wanting the ACA repealed, sincerely believing that the detriments exceeded the benefits of the law. By contrast, however, Trump made it clear that his goal was to hurt real people, to advance something that he himself was not able to articulate.

After the GOP efforts failed, Trump threatened to cut Obamacare's cost-sharing subsidies once again, and insurers would probably flee the exchanges in 2018, if not before, leaving millions of Americans without any options for subsidized coverage in the individual market. Insurers rely on the subsidies, referred to as cost-sharing reduction payments, to lower the deductibles and co-pays of low income enrollees. Nearly six million enrollees qualified for the cost-sharing payments in 2017. Paid directly to insurers, the subsidies were expected to cost the federal government about $7 billion in 2017.[7] Trump repeatedly threatened to cut off the payments and ignored the request from insurers, healthcare providers, governors and others to guarantee that the payments will be made for the time being. Because of the threats of letting Obamacare implode, an August 2017 analysis by the non-partisan Kaiser Family Foundation found the administration's actions would trigger double-digit premium increases on health insurance policies purchased by many consumers.[8]

Did Trump take any blame for the spectacular crash and burn or increased premiums? Did he consider that perhaps he should work with Democrats and work out something that would work for all Americans? No. His strategy simply became to let Obamacare fail. "*We're not going to own it. I'm not going to own it. I can tell you the Republicans are not going to own it. We'll let Obamacare fail and then the Democrats are going to come to us,"* Trump told reporters at the White House on July 17, 2017. That's not leadership.

Trump made good on his promise on October 12, 2017 in two different ways. First, he signed an executive order that would push people into what were previously called "junk" insurance plans that he claimed would lower costs and provide more options. The order would make it easier for small businesses to purchase insurance through "association health plans," which businesses could create. However, many patients, doctors, hospitals, and regulators claimed that the order could increase costs for sick people, greatly increase the number of "bare-bones" plans and add additional uncertainty to health insurance markets.

A few hours later, Trump stopped funding for the cost-sharing subsidies. The answer is not yet clear what this means to the six million people who receive these subsidies but in the short-term, insurers will have to continue providing the cost-sharing discounts even though the government will no longer reimburse them. Premiums are expected to greatly increase.

No one ever claimed that Obamacare was not flawed. Obama himself frequently encouraged lawmakers to come up with a better plan and if Republicans were able, or are able, to do so, that would be a victory for everyone. Joe Biden acknowledged what everybody knows, that *"The ACA isn't perfect,"* but pointed out the philosophy behind the law. *"The choices we made when designing the law flowed from a commitment to provide the best possible care to the most people."*[9] I, too, acknowledge the many flaws of the ACA, but the remedy is for the parties to work together to fix it, not dismantle it for the sole purpose of scoring political points.

After the multiple failed attempts to replace and repeal Obamacare, Congress passed a tax bill signed into law on December 22, 2017 by the president that will, among other things, affect healthcare in America.

"*I shouldn't say this,*" Trump said while taking a victory lap, "*but we essentially repealed Obamacare.*" While that statement was, as usual, an inaccurate hyperbole, the tax bill eliminated the individual mandate, the engine that made the Affordable Care Act work, throwing the healthcare system into chaos without providing an alternative remedy. During a Cabinet meeting, the president said, "*Obamacare has been repealed in this bill. We didn't want to bring it up. I told people specifically, 'Be quiet with the fake-news media because I don't want them talking too much about it.'*" It's not clear whether Trump truly understood what he was saying but, for better or worse, he essentially admitted paternity for the healthcare system and the consequences that will ensue.

While the mandate was unpopular with many, it was meant as an incentive so younger, healthier people who may not think they need health insurance would get coverage. It was also meant to be a way to make people not wait until they are sick to buy insurance. Health insurance companies need healthy people in a pool with sick people because it's prohibitively expensive to cover only sick people. Insurance companies have already said that without the mandate, they'll have to raise premiums and pass on other costs to people who do have health insurance.

It's impossible to predict everything that will happen on healthcare in 2018 and beyond, but one thing is clear: healthcare affects every single American and comprises one-sixth of the economy. Quickly enacting "solutions" by one party without thorough deliberation, extensive hearings and the input of the other party simply to achieve a political victory is not the solution. Such short-sightedness will only guarantee a rollercoaster ride of ups and downs, changes and reversals, as elections come and go. There must be a better way.

Healthcare, perhaps more than any other aspect of society, illustrates the shortcomings in our partisan system. There are no easy answers but the best solution is to fix the ACA in a bi-partisan fashion with Democrats and Republicans working together. Keep the things that work, change the things that don't. Stop making this a Democratic versus a Republican thing; *it's an American thing.* The House Republicans started dancing prematurely when they passed the *AHCA* while Democrats immaturely started singing, "Hey, hey, goodbye," implying that Republicans would be gone in 2018. Our citizens deserve better. Democrats will fashion remedies differently than Republicans but when our loved ones get sick, we all want access to good healthcare that will help them get better.

NOW WHAT?

A January 2017 Pew Research Center poll showed, for the first time in history, that most Americans, 60%, believe it is the government's responsibility to ensure access to quality healthcare.[10] The fate of the Obamacare repeal could have been predicted since a majority of people didn't want it repealed but merely fixed and improved. Mitch McConnell and Paul Ryan tried to get healthcare the same way the Democrats had in 2010, without the participation of the other party, but that didn't work.

Because of Trump's threats and actions to let Obamacare implode, "single-payer" suddenly started to gather steam. During the 2016 campaign, Hillary Clinton dismissed single-payer as something that would never come to pass. However, one year later, all of the 2020 Democratic presidential hopefuls started getting behind the "Medicare for All" (a.k.a. single-payer) health-care bill championed by Sen. Bernie Sanders. All of this suggests the dam is breaking when it comes to government-run healthcare, at least for Democrats. Despite critics of single-payer, the writing seems to be on the wall. However, one big question remains:

Who will pay for it?

The only other option is for the two parties to try to find an answer on a non-partisan basis and use conservative principles that work well and mix them with more liberal positions. After the collapse of the Senate healthcare bill, former Presidential candidate John Kasich wrote an op-ed in the *Washington Post* about going forward, presenting other options as well. Before getting into specifics, he hit the nail on the head by addressing the process problem and the toxic partisanship.

> *"Washington's approach to healthcare over the past decade is yet another example of our lawmakers' increasing distance from the rest of America. First, one party rams through a rigid, convoluted plan that drives up costs though unsustainable mechanisms that are now unraveling. Then, the other party pursues fixes that go too far the other way — and again ignores ideas from the other side. Neither extreme is cutting it and the quick opposition that doomed the Senate plan reflects how unacceptable its ideas are to so many. The American people want and deserve reasonable, balanced healthcare so that they can live without the fear of bankruptcy if they get sick, our most vulnerable neighbors are treated with compassion, and those who seek to improve their lives can get healthy, confront addiction, and get work."* [11]

Healthcare is too important to make a partisan issue. Let the two parties work together and make the American healthcare system the best in the world.

STAGGERING

For several agonizing minutes during the last 400 meters of the women's marathon in the 1984 Summer Olympics, millions of viewers were wondering not whether Switzerland's Gabriela Andersen would finish, but whether she would survive. Andersen came out of the dark Coliseum tunnel lurching, seemingly being pulled off the track by some unseen force. Track stewards followed her, as she staggered away, fearing they would touch her and disqualify her.

Her final lap seemed to take forever as she staggered, appearing drunk, veering across lanes, her head and shoulders bent forward. As she approached the finish line, her pace increased and her right arm began swinging wildly. Finally crossing the finish line, she collapsed into the arms of stewards. A fierce medical debate ensued afterwards and it was concluded that Anderson had suffered from heat prostration, or mild dehydration, and not the more serious heatstroke.

Millions of Americans have no health insurance or inadequate health insurance and, like Anderson, find themselves staggering. It's easy to say that's their problem. Besides the moral issues, health insurance for all would result in a more productive society. That should be a goal that on which Republicans and Democrats should be able to agree. Just like with a football team, you cannot only care for a few. Every player, regardless of talent or ability, must be cared for. Anything less is wrong.

7

ENEMIES

"America will never be destroyed from the outside. If we falter and lose our freedoms, it will be because we destroyed ourselves."
Abraham Lincoln

"Here on earth you will have many trials and sorrows. But take heart because I have overcome the world."
Jesus in John 16:33

"Goldfish and hamsters and white mice and even the little seed in the Styrofoam cup all die. So do we."
All I Really Need to Know I learned in Kindergarten

Unheralded Pat Tillman from Arizona State was selected in the 1998 NFL draft by the Arizona Cardinals and started ten games in his first season. In May 2002, after completing the remaining games after the 9/11 attacks, Tillman turned down a contract offer of $3.6 million over three years from the Cardinals to enlist in the Army with his brother Kevin. After seeing action in Iraq in September 2003, they went back to Georgia to attend Ranger School and both graduated on November 28, 2003.

Tillman was subsequently redeployed to Afghanistan, but on April 22, 2004, he was killed. The Army initially claimed that Tillman and his unit were attacked in an ambush. It wasn't until after his burial that investigations were launched, eventually ruling that friendly fire was the cause of his death

The world is a dangerous place and the United States faces daunting challenges all over the globe. While a football team needs a quarterback who can throw the ball and receivers who can score touchdowns, you need a strong defense. When the opponent moves the ball inside the so-called red zone, a tough defense becomes even more important.

The primary task for any president is to ensure that the country is safe from would-be enemies. We must be ever vigilant. We cannot ever let the enemy get into the red zone, as Al-Qaeda did on September 11, 2001. While the United States is the strongest country ever to exist, rockets and tanks alone do not a great country make.

No one really knew what to expect in foreign relations from the new administration because Trump came into office with few stated positions on foreign policy except the vague promise to put "America first." His campaign promised to "bomb the s---" out of ISIS, fill Guantanamo with "bad dudes," and return to waterboarding and a "hell of a lot worse," but such proclamations do not exactly make a cohesive foreign policy. He wanted to improve relations with Russia despite the unanimous assessment of the U.S. intelligence community of its interference in the presidential election. He attacked alliances, implied that we would come to the defense of attacked NATO allies only if they contributed more on defense, vowed to tear up or renegotiate several international agreements, pledged to end "nation-building" missions, and promised a massive buildup in the size of the military, although that has yet to happen.

Beyond predicting that Trump will most likely continue belittling allies and enemies alike on Twitter, and making false statements, it will be hard to anticipate what the future holds in 2018 and beyond. While there are many aspects of foreign policy, only a few are addressed here: terrorism, North Korea, Iran and Russian interference in our election.

TERRORISM

The U.S. has no choice but to fight and defeat ISIS. In the long run, military force alone will not be enough, as economic inequality and alienation will not be overcome by weapons and troops. Policies of engagement must be pursued. Just as cultural programs in Europe after World War II helped to build bridges to the Muslim world, similar programs should be seen as an investment in the future. To be sure, ISIS represents a real threat. We cannot negotiate with ISIS. We must kill them, but we must also reverse the rate of failed states that lead to conditions where young men are willing to kill themselves. ISIS recruits alienated young men by convincing them that Muslims everywhere are under assault from the West. Weak governments, porous borders, and civil conflict all contribute to recruitment.

Terrorism in general, and ISIS in particular, is not just a military threat. If it were, it would have been defeated by now. Communism was also not defeated by military force alone. According to Vaclav Havel, the first president of the Czech Republic, "*Communism was not defeated by military force but by life, by the human spirit, by conscience, by the resistance of man to manipulation.*"[1] It was defeated, former Secretary of State Madeleine Albright said, because those who opposed it were able to expose its lies and we must do the same.

During the 2016 campaign, Donald Trump claimed that he had a secret plan to defeat the Islamic State and bragged that he knew more about ISIS than the generals did. Despite those criticisms, the Trump Administration's policy to defeat ISIS is essentially the same as the Obama Administration and is being carried out mostly by the same people. The Obama approach, which Trump ridiculed, was to work with and through partners in Iraq and Syria. This plan continues, as does the campaign of air strikes and targeted raids by the U.S. and the coalition. Also unchanged is the arming, training, and advising of local partners, backed by a small number of U.S. troops on the ground. The primary objectives – seizing Mosul in Iraq, Raqqa in Syria, and countering ISIS elements in southern Syria and the Euphrates valley – did not change.

The Obama plan was roundly criticized by Trump as being ineffective, weak, and practically treasonous. While partisanship is unavoidable to some extent, it cannot be the dominant force in foreign and national security policy. President Obama concluded, and President Trump apparently agrees, that the current approach is the most effective and the most likely to accomplish our objectives. The current plan is working and has yielded results with steady gains of territory once controlled by ISIS, including Mosul in July of 2017 and Raqqa in October 2017. Trump has stuck with a plan he once blasted, although he continually claims credit for its success, even tweeting in April 2018, "The United States, under my administration, has done a great job of ridding the region of ISIS. Where is our 'Thank you, America?'"

NORTH KOREA

North Korea, which is run by an immature egomaniac, is without a doubt the biggest threat to the United States. In July of 2017, it successfully tested an intercontinental ballistic missile capable of reaching the United States. It is not quite there yet, but is very close. President Trump previously said this would not happen on his watch, but it has. While there is no perfect plan to deal with a lunatic like Kim Jong-Un, Trump repeatedly shocked the world by repeatedly engaging in provocative and belligerent name-calling and insults and then stunned friend and foe alike when he accepted an invitation in March 2018 to meet with the reclusive North Korean.

On many occasions, President Trump suggested a willingness to take unilateral military action. *"If China is not going to solve North Korea, we will. That is all I am telling you."* In April 2017, Trump, speaking to Reuters, contradicted his secretary of state. *"There is a chance that we could end up having a major, major conflict with North Korea. Absolutely."*

During the back and forth of the comments described above, much of the world was not really paying attention. That changed on August 8, 2017 when Trump threatened North Korea with *"fire and fury."* Over the course of the next few days, Trump and Kim exchanged threats as they battled to see who was the toughest guy on the playground and Trump said if North Korea issued anymore threats, it would face something *"the likes of which the world has never seen."* The problem, of course, with such proclamations is that if the U.S. doesn't act whenever North Korea makes a threat, Trump's chest-thumping will be exposed as empty words.

The war of words between Trump and Kim continued to escalate and speaking before the U.N. General Assembly in September 2017, Trump said:

> *"The United States has great strength and patience, but if it is forced to defend itself or its allies, it will have no choice but to totally destroy North Korea. Rocket Man is on a suicide mission for himself and his regime."*

In response, North Korea compared the speech to a barking dog and Kim took the unprecedented step of personally responding to Trump:

"Whatever Trump might have expected, he will face results beyond his expectation. I will surely and definitely tame the mentally deranged U.S. dotard with fire."

Although most Americans did not know what a "dotard" was, Trump's response was to make the juvenile term "Rocket Man" an even more junior-high-ish "Little Rocket Man" and to call Kim a "madman." Trump also said that North Korea *"won't be around much longer."* And on October 6, 2017, Trump, in a photo-op with military commanders and their spouses, called in reporters and said, *"You guys know what this represents? Maybe it's the calm before the storm?"* A reporter asked, *"What storm, Mr. President?"*[2] He just smiled and said nothing. Since no storm ever came, it is clear that the statement was a hollow attempt to provoke or create a stir. If it wasn't so serious, it would be comical.

While the Pentagon may have a plan to pre-emptively destroy North Korea's nuclear capacity, and while new national security advisor John Bolton has been known to favor such action, the likely outcome would be catastrophic. Hundreds of thousands, or even millions, of America's allies, and thousands of American troops and dependents could be killed, South Korea could permanently turn against the U.S. and the Chinese might intervene. It could also convince other American allies that the U.S. is completely unreliable and can no longer be trusted. Moreover, if the United States was totally preoccupied with North Korea, that would mean that Russia, China, and ISIS could operate more freely than before.

North Korea is a serious problem with no obvious solution. Despite the achievement of a unanimous vote in the U.N. Security Council strengthening economic sanctions against North Korea, Trump made several significant mistakes. First, his blustering threat of "fire and fury" was absurd. Presidents should not make threats unless they plan to execute them. Secondly, similar to what President Obama did in Syria, Trump mistakenly drew a red line in the sand. Third, his bellicose threat at the

U.N. to "totally destroy" North Korea unnecessarily worsened relations and exacerbated the chances of a nuclear war.

Besides strengthening our military position, the U.S. should commit to diplomatically containing North Korea's nuclear program. It's not an accident that every president since Eisenhower has never threatened the use of nuclear weapons. We need to retain the moral high ground and persuade the rest of the world to help us against an international outlaw. While there are no guarantees with diplomacy, it would be reckless and irresponsible not to try. Sudden and unilateral U.S. military action, which is appealing because it looks "tough," could trigger a catastrophic conflict with massive loss of civilian life.

The U.S. must find a way to unite South Korea, Japan, Russia, and China to pressure North Korea to stop its nuclear and ballistic missile tests. It would be inexcusable for an American president to go to war without having at least given diplomacy a chance. This is easier said than done, however, because Trump hasn't made diplomacy a priority. He has threatened to drastically cut the State Department budget and has routinely ignored the career Foreign Service. Only 61 out of 154 positions at the State Department needing Senate confirmation had been filled by the end of 2017[2] and many key positions, such as the Ambassador post to South Korea, don't even have a nominee.[3] Trump seemingly doesn't care and when asked about it gave this incredible answer: *I'm the only one that matters.*

Notwithstanding the above, brand new problems were created when Trump abruptly decided in March 2018 to meet with Kim, on the same day that he suddenly decided to increase tariffs. Not only were allies not consulted, Trump's top advisors were not either, showing once again Trump's impulsiveness. Moments after he accepted the invitation, facilitated by South Korean diplomats visiting the White House, Trump popped into the White House briefing room to alert journalists of a major announcement. "Hopefully, you will give me credit," the president said gleefully. It's hard to follow how we could go from 70 years of animosity and threats of totally destroying North Korea to sitting down for a cozy summit. The moment the two leaders meet and stand together as equals, however, North Korea will take seize the advantage since for decades they have craved international respect and credibility. Secondly, by accepting so quickly, the U.S. received nothing in exchange. Almost nobody expects what the White House is demanding: total denuclearization on the Korean peninsula. It's entirely possible that Kim believes denuclearization to mean a withdrawal of the U.S. nuclear umbrella, and perhaps even the withdrawal of American forces, from South Korea. If the summit turns out to be merely a photo-op without any verifiable pledge by North Korea to eliminate its nukes, the meeting will be seen as a crushing failure to U.S. credibility.

Thirdly, since we don't know what Kim's expectations are, a failed summit could make things worse and trigger escalations on both sides and serve as an excuse for war. And lastly, how can we possibly trust them? Two days after the sudden announcement, Trump tweeted, *"North Korea has not conducted a Missile Test since November 28, 2017 and has promised not to do so through our meetings. I believe they will honor that commitment."*

Since the North Koreans have repeatedly violated the terms of past agreements, how could the president possibly make such a declaration with any degree of accuracy? And how can he distinguish the sudden trust in Kim with his frequent denunciations of Iran as being untrustworthy? Trump mercilessly attacked Barack Obama for naively negotiating with the Iranians. After repeatedly threatening North Korea with annihilation, how can we possibly trust them or expect them to negotiate in good faith?

If North Korea actually destroys its nuclear weapons, Trump will deserve credit and I will be the first to admit it. But most experts believe the summit is a trap that Trump agreed to only because he doesn't understand history or policy and doesn't worry about long-term ramifications. Leading the free world by impulsively living only in the moment is frightening.

IRAN

In 2015, Iran was very close to producing a nuclear weapon. Years in the making, a deal was reached with Iran whereby money seized decades ago by the U.S. was released to Iran in exchange for their agreement to halt their nuclear program and allow inspection by the IAEA. Many people vigorously objected to the agreement, including President Trump. However, while Iran is a headache, a nuclear-armed Iran is a nightmare that cannot be allowed to happen.

Ever since the Islamic Revolution of 1979, Iran has been a rogue nation and so many opposed the agreement reached with Iran and the U.S., Russia, England, China, France, and Germany (not just the U.S.), including President Trump. Most criticisms don't address the agreement itself but focus on Iran's untrustworthiness, the possibility of more terrorism and American hostages. All valid points. The issues are extremely complex and while the agreement is imperfect and was negotiated by flawed people, it comes down to two things: 1) A nuclear Iran is unthinkable, and 2) what's the alternative? As one negotiator put it, "*We didn't cure cancer. But we'll limit Iran's ability to build a nuclear weapon.*" The next to last thing the U.S. needs at this time is another war in the Middle East. The last thing the United States needs, and the entire world for that matter, is a nuclear war in the Middle East.

On October 13, 2017, Trump accused Iran of committing multiple violations of the agreement, despite the fact that the International Atomic Energy Association, America's European allies, and even his own government said that Tehran was complying with the 2015 agreement (Secretary of Defense James Mattis testified before Congress that it is in

America's best interests to stay in the agreement[4]). Trump said that he would no longer make regular certifications, as the agreement requires the president to do every 90 days, that the lifting of sanctions under the deal was in the best interest of the United States, kicking the matter over to Congress to decide in 60 days whether or not to re-impose sanctions. If he did not get the changes he wanted, Trump said, he would walk away from the deal.

As a result of these sanctions, Iran's economy has been crippled for decades and, in many ways, Iran is a failed state. While it is tempting to think they deserve it and that it will prevent them from engaging in terrorism, the opposite is true. Failed states, where there is no stable economy, legal system or political structure, and where millions of young men have no jobs, breed terrorism. Al-Qaeda was not in Iraq when the U.S. arrived in 2003 but appeared during the subsequent instability that arose. The U.S. will benefit immensely, as will all the world, if Iran becomes a stable member of the international community. Will that happen? Maybe not. Maybe Iran will continue its nefarious ways. If that happens, the agreement can be negated.

Killing this deal will not help American or Western security and will further isolate the United States. It will not help the demonstrators who have taken to the street and, in fact, will strengthen the mullahs who have laid the blame for the demonstrations at the feet of the U.S. The powerful Revolutionary Guard was able to mostly suppress the protests and a re-imposition of sanctions will deliver a mortal blow to efforts to revive support for a return of democracy. It will compromise our relations with our European allies. Lastly, it will give new strength to Russia and China and, since Iran and Russia signed agreements in November 2017 to collaborate on energy worth as much as $30 billion, it will result in the loss of American jobs.[5]

But with the selection of John Bolton in March 2018 as Trump's new national security advisor, the chances that the U.S. will kill the deal have greatly increased, since the hawkish Bolton has argued that preemptive strikes against North Korea and Iran would be justified.

RUSSIA

The Trump Administration has been hobbled by the issue of Russian meddling almost since day one and special prosecutor Robert Mueller was appointed by the Trump Justice Department to determine what happened. Mueller has acted aggressively, sending the FBI in on a before-dawn raid on July 26, 2017 on the house of Trump's former campaign manager, Paul Manafort, and then indicting Manafort on October 30, 2017. On the same day, former aide George Papadopoulos pled guilty, followed by former National Security Adviser Michael Flynn in December 2017 and then Manafort's key deputy, Rick Gates, followed by the indictment of 13 Russian nationals. The Mueller investigation is still going strong in 2018, with no end in sight, something that has infuriated Trump and his allies. It even expanded into another jurisdiction, the Southern District of New York, with a stunning FBI raid on Trump's personal attorney, Michael Cohen, in April. After initially cooperating with the special counsel, Trump's team began a concerted effort to attack Mueller and his team as being biased and tainted. It is impossible to predict where the Russia investigation will end up but it is clear that the partisan divide that exists will grow wider.

Whether or not Manafort or others are convicted, or whether or not Trump or his associates colluded, it is monumental that a foreign adversary interfered in our election. Trump has consistently resisted any investigation into finding out how this happened and how to prevent it in the future, presumably since it might delegitimize his win. He has done everything in his power to label the entire investigation a "hoax" and "witch hunt" perpetrated by Democrats angered at their electoral loss. However, his refusal to take action demonstrates that every issue confronting America is viewed by him as to how it relates to him personally.

The issue of whether the Russians interfered is without dispute. Trump's secretary of state, defense secretary, CIA director, national security advisor, U.N. Ambassador, and Director of National Intelligence have all acknowledged the interference. Yet Trump is apparently unable or unwilling to admit this interference, claiming repeatedly that it is just a big hoax perpetrated by Democrats upset about losing the election. Standing on foreign soil during the 2017 G-20 meeting in Hamburg, Trump rejected the unanimous conclusion of his own intelligence community and said, "*No one really knows.*"

Besides the investigation headed up by Special Counsel Robert Mueller, several Russia investigations were undertaken by various Congressional committees. Although they all promised to work in a bipartisan fashion, they predictably fell victim to tribalism. The Republicans on the House Intelligence Committee issued findings after a secret session without the input from the committee Democrats that there was no collusion. Incredibly, they also came to the conclusion that the professionals in the intelligence community were wrong when they determined that Russian interference was carried out with the specific desire to help Trump and hurt Clinton although they offered no tangible evidence. The Democrats, after numerous unsuccessful attempts to issue subpoenas, interview more witnesses and call back witnesses whose testimony was later shown to be untruthful or incomplete, pledged to keep investigating but the juvenile partisanship made the entire endeavor a total waste of time.

It was inevitable that the House Committee would fail to make any finding against the president as its chairman Devon Nunes, according to Fox News Judith Miller, was "President Trump's faithful lapdog"-or his "stooge" for doing, as his hometown *Fresno Bee* called him, the White House's "dirty work." Nunes, Miller wrote, "is serving the interests of his real boss, President Trump, rather than those of his constituents. He is also undermining true conservative values."[6] Nunes had previously authored a memo that purported to show that the FISA Court warrant allowing surveillance of former Trump associate Carter Page in October of 2016 was politically motivated. For weeks, Trump supporters demanded to "Release the Memo," believing that it would prove Trump innocent, despite the fact that Page was no longer with the campaign when the warrant was obtained and was renewed several times by several FISA judges, all Republican appointees. One of the several applications was even approved by Trump's own deputy attorney general. Although the memo fizzled when it came out for its lack of substance, Trump incredibly agreed to release it over vigorous objections of his own Justice Department. When the Democrats issued a memo of their own, Trump blocked its release.

After the Republicans shut down their probe, Trump gleefully tweeted that he had been exonerated. But it was clear to everyone that this finding was political pure and simple. The Center for American Progress's ("CAP") Moscow Project concluded that the Committee simply didn't try very hard, finding that the Committee did not obtain complete information from 81% of the known contacts between Trump officials and Russians. The report confirmed at least 70 contacts between the Trump team and Russia operatives in the year before Trump took office and pointed out that the Committee failed to interview key witnesses in 60% of the cases.[7] Many witnesses, such as Steve Bannon, appeared before the Committee and refused to answer questions. The Committee Chairman fussed and complained and threatened contempt but in the end did nothing. It appears unlikely that Congress will ever find fault with a Republican president, no matter what evidence may exist.

Whether or not there was collusion between the Trump campaign and the Russians, it is "incontrovertible," as H.R. McMaster put it, that the Russians meddled. And yet, the U.S. has taken limited action in response.

Until March 2018, the president blocked the implementation of sanctions that had overwhelmingly been approved by Congress months earlier. In March 2018, the *New York Times* reported that the State Department had not yet spent one penny of the $120 million that it had been allocated to counter the Russian interference.[8] In shocking testimony before Congress in March, NSA Director Admiral Michael Rogers admitted that the U.S. had not adequately responded to Russian meddling and that the president had never directed him or other top officials to take any specific actions.[9]

In a February 2018 article, the *Washington Post* asked its readers to imagine.

> *"Imagine if, after 9/11, the president had said that the World Trade Center and Pentagon could have been attacked by China or 'lots of other people.' Imagine if he had dismissed the claims of Al-Qaeda's responsibility as a 'hoax' and that he 'really believed' Osama bin Laden's denials. Imagine if he saw the attack primarily as a political embarrassment to be minimized rather than as a national security threat to be combated... That's roughly where we stand after the second-worst attack on America in the past two decades."* [10]

Whether you are a Democrat or Republican, America was attacked for a hostile adversary and our failure to respond adequately is inexcusable.

It is also clear that the U.S. government has taken very few, if any, measures to protect the elections of 2018 and 2020. Senator Ben Cardin of the Senate Foreign Relations Committee issued a report on January 10, 2018 that claims the U.S. will not be prepared to defend against possible Russian meddling in the 2018 midterm elections or the 2020 presidential contest unless it takes action immediately. The report warns that the Russians will act more aggressively unless the U.S. counters the threat. The report puts the onus on the president, stating: "*Without leadership from the President, any attempt to marshal such a response will be inherently weakened at the outset... President Trump has been negligent in acknowledging and responding to the threat to U.S. national security posed by Putin's meddling."*[11]

The report calls for the following actions to be taken: 1) The establishment of a high-level inter-agency group to coordinate U.S. policy in connection with Russian operations; 2) a comprehensive strategy to deal with all aspects of Russia's tactics to be presented to Congress; 3) holding social media companies such as Facebook and Twitter more accountable; 4) the issuance of a new sanctions designation called "state hybrid threat actors" for countries that use destabilizing tactics such as cyberwarfare against other nations; 5) a more personal targeting of Putin's "personal corruption and wealth stored abroad;" 6) a plan to assist European allies to reduce their dependence on Russian energy supplies.[12]

There have been many attempts by the administration to downplay the Russian meddling or to paint it simply as a Democratic hoax. The evidence is overwhelming and other nations understand. England has taken steps to strengthen its cybersecurity and electoral processes. Germany has issued a strong warning to Russia that there will be consequences if there is meddling in its elections. Spain has cracked down on Russian organized crime and France has engaged in a coordinated effort to dilute Russian hacking. Smaller countries have also taken steps, leaving the U.S. as about the only country in the world that does not consider Russian meddling into its elections as a serious offense. This is not a tribal issue; this is not a Democrat or Republican thing. A foreign power attacked us and will continue to do so. We must find out what happened in 2016 and prevent it from happening again.

DREAM TEAM

Until the 1992 Olympic Games, only amateur players were allowed to play. However, the Eastern-Bloc's state-sponsored "full-time amateur athlete" made a mockery of the pure amateur and put Western countries at a disadvantage since Soviet athletes were essentially paid by the state to train on a full-time basis. The 1988 U.S. men's team, made up of college stars, finished in third place, a humiliating result for the country that invented basketball. As a result, the 1992 team included, for the first time, professional players from the NBA. That team, which included Michael Jordan, Larry Bird, and Magic Johnson, was dubbed the Dream Team and is widely considered the greatest team ever assembled.

The American military must always be the best and we must strive to constantly have a "dream team." We must do everything possible to defeat and destroy ISIS. We must find a solution to the North Korea problem, we must prevent Iran from getting a nuclear weapon and we must find out how Russia interfered with our election.

We have enemies who want to do us harm and we must vigilantly defend against those who wish America and its allies ill. We must use our unparalleled military in concert with our allies and in conjunction with education, foreign aid, and diplomacy. "Fire and fury" may sound tough, but it is counterproductive, foolish, and boxes the U.S. into a corner where the only option is nuclear war. Military defense and foreign policy are not partisan issues and all Americans, whether Democrat or Republican, should be able to agree that politics stop at the water's edge.

OFFENSE

8

CLIMATE

"I am a slow walker but I never walk back."
Abraham Lincoln

"I have been given all authority in heaven and on earth."
Jesus, Matthew 28:18

"Flush."
All I Really Need to Know I Learned in Kindergarten

The 1967 NFC Championship game between the Dallas Cowboys and the Green Bay Packers, one of the most famous games in NFL history, was dubbed "The Ice Bowl." The game-time temperature at Lambeau Field was –15 °F, with an average wind chill of –48 °F. The turf-heating system malfunctioned and when the tarpaulin was removed, the field flash-froze. The University of Wisconsin-La Crosse band performed but the mouthpieces of brass instruments got stuck to the players' lips and seven members of the band were treated for hypothermia. During the game, an elderly spectator in the stands died from exposure.

As referee Norm Schachter blew his metal whistle to start the game, it froze to his lips. Trying to free the whistle, the skin ripped off and his lips began to bleed. For the rest of the game, the officials used voice commands to officiate. At one point, CBS announcer Frank Gifford famously said on air, *"I'm going to take a bite of my coffee."*

Down 17-14, the Packers took over possession with 4:50 left. With the wind chill at –70 °F, quarterback Bart Starr led his team to the Dallas two-foot line. With 16 seconds remaining, Starr lunged across the goal line for the win. Several players suffered frostbite, including Packers Linebacker Ray Nitschke, who developed it in his feet, causing his toenails to fall off and his toes to turn purple.

Every aspect of our lives is affected by the weather, including professional football games. If you live in a cold area, you get used to bundling up during the winter and if you live in a warm area, you get used to that as well. It's no big deal, but climate change is literally a threat to our existence, although not everyone agrees.

PITTSBURGH, NOT PARIS

On June 1, 2017, President Trump did what he had long threatened to do. Standing in the Rose Garden, packed with reporters, activists and supporters, as a military band played soft jazz, he withdrew the U.S. from the Paris Climate Agreement. *"I was elected to represent the citizens of Pittsburgh, not Paris,"* Trump said to cheers. Under the Agreement, entered into by the entire world save Syria and Nicaragua, the U.S. had pledged to reduce its greenhouse gas emissions 26 to 28% below 2005 levels by 2025 and contribute several billion dollars in aid to poorer countries by 2020.[1] I believe this decision will not only be immensely harmful to the

United States, but that it will cede global leadership to others and greatly reduce our influence.

Our withdrawal will result in less influence in the world for the U.S., diminish our national security, and will actually cost American jobs. Trump's vision of bringing back coal and mining jobs is backwards and he fails to understand the great potential for jobs in the renewable energy arena. As reported in the *New York Times* on June 1, 2017:

> *"Mr. Trump's decision to abandon the agreement for environmental action signed by 195 nations is a remarkable rebuke to heads of state, climate activists, corporate executives, and members of the president's own staff, who all failed to change his mind with an intense, last-minute lobbying blitz. The Paris Agreement was intended to bind the world community into battling rising temperatures in concert and the departure of the Earth's second largest polluter is a major blow."* [2]

As with healthcare, there is a threshold question, which is this: is global warming real or is it, as Trump has said repeatedly, a hoax? During his announcement, Trump said, *"We are getting out, but we will start to negotiate and we will see if we can make a deal that's fair."* However, if it's a hoax, then why would the U.S. try to renegotiate?

Very few believe that global warming is a hoax. Within minutes of Trump's announcement, the leaders of France, Germany, and Italy issued a statement that the Paris Agreement was "irreversible" and could not be renegotiated. The EU's Commissioner for climate said, *"Today's announcement has galvanized us rather than weakened us and this vacuum will be filled by new broad committed leadership."* Thirty-four states, including California and New York, are continuing with ambitious carbon reduction plans, while the CEOs of General Electric and Goldman Sachs and others said the withdrawal would be a surrender of clean energy jobs of the future to other countries while Elon Musk of

Tesla, a member of two business-related councils that the president had established, announced that he was leaving the panels. *"Climate change is real. Leaving Paris is not good for America or the world."*[3]

"At what point does America get demeaned? At what point do they start laughing at us as a country?" Trump asked during his announcement. *"We don't want other leaders and other countries laughing at us anymore. And they won't be."* The truth is, however, that the rest of the world is laughing at us. Trump's reasoning is hard to understand since there was never any binding international agreement and America's compliance was completely voluntary. Nobody in Paris or Brussels or London was interfering with American sovereignty. The only apparent explanation was that Trump was making good on a campaign promise to eliminate practically everything that Obama had enacted. The objective was political, not substantive.

While over-regulation can sometimes impede the economy, I do not understand the concerted effort to harm the environment, the American worker, and our national security. The debate is always framed as a choice between protecting the spotted owl or growing the economy. You can have industrial growth, some will say, but you can't have it and clean air at the same time. That's false. Moreover, this debate cannot be limited to only current taxpayers since many decisions will affect our country for generations. Lastly, Trump's premise, which is that leaving the agreement will create jobs, is flat wrong. Trump wants to protect jobs in the oil, gas, and coal industries, but the better course of action would be to invest in clean energy industries that will create more long-term employment. Trump wants to bring America back to a place that is no longer there. The decision to withdraw will not benefit Americans in any way, will hurt us globally, and will harm future generations. It's a lose-lose-lose proposition.

BURY SCIENCE?

On August 7, 2017, worried that President Trump and EPA administrator Scott Pruitt would suppress their findings, a group of scientists from 13 federal agencies took the amazing step of leaking a draft of a sweeping climate change study before the Administration had approved it.[4] The EPA and other agencies must sign off on the report, which, if released, would be part of the National Climate Assessment, due for release in 2018.

The study concluded that global warming is getting worse, that significant action must be taken and that global temperatures are expected to rise significantly over the next century, setting up yet another clash between administration officials and government scientists. Some believe that the White House is trying to bury science related to global warming.

> *"Evidence for a changing climate abounds, from the top of the atmosphere to the depths of the oceans," a portion of the study reads. "Many lines of evidence demonstrate that human activities, especially emissions of greenhouse gases, are primarily responsible for recent observed climate change."* [5]

The fact that scientists operated from a presumption that the president would bury their work and that they had to leak it to ensure that it saw the light of day is mind-boggling. Government scientists concluded that humans are harming the environment and they had to leak the report because they did not trust the president. Chew on that for a while.

Two weeks after the leak, the Trump Administration decided to disband the federal advisory panel for the National Climate Assessment. The committee was created to help translate findings from the National Climate Assessment into concrete guidance for both public and private-sector officials. While many state and local officials have sought guidance from Washington on how to factor climate change into future infrastructure, the administration has proceeded the opposite way. Seattle mayor Ed Murray said that the move to dissolve the climate advisory committee represents *"the president stepping away from reality."*

In the year before Hurricane Harvey struck the Gulf Coast in August 2017, the daily surface temperature of the Gulf of Mexico was always above 73 degrees, something that had never happened before.[6] Experts agree that heavier rainfall is caused by warmer weather because when the seas warm, more moisture evaporates and when the air warms, it can carry more moisture. While President Trump will no doubt dispute it, Harvey and Irma's unprecedented destruction is almost certainly related to climate change.

"The heaviest rainfall events have become heavier and more frequent, and the amount of rain falling on the heaviest rain days has also increased," said the National Climate Assessment. *"The mechanism driving these changes,"* is hotter air stemming from *"human-caused warming."*[7] Instead of burying our heads in the sand, let's use these horrible storms to embark upon a national effort to reduce carbon emissions.

NATIONAL SECURITY

If you don't care about the environment for its beauty, or because we were commanded by God to be stewards of the earth, protecting the environment is a huge national security issue. Foreign policy experts, like former Under Secretary of State R. Nicholas Burns, are concerned that U.S. withdrawal from the Paris accord will affect U.S. influence on many diplomatic issues. Several members of the Council on Foreign Relations believe the decision *"will endanger U.S. national security and prosperity by sabotaging U.S. global leadership and will allow China to fill the leadership vacuum."*[8]

On September 21, 2016, the Obama Administration issued a report from the National Intelligence Council (NIC) which confirmed that climate change has already created national security challenges for the United States and other countries and will continue to do so for the next 20 years. These challenges are: 1) Threats to the stability of countries, 2) heightened social and political tensions, 3) adverse effects on food prices and availability, 4) increased risks to human health, 5) negative impacts on investments and economic competitiveness, and 6) potential climate discontinuities and secondary surprises.[9]

Shiloh Fetzek, Senior Fellow for International Affairs at the Center for Climate and Security, emphasized that climate change has geo-political consequences.

> *"The actions and priorities outlined in these documents lay the groundwork for the next Administration to continue to address this non-partisan security issue robustly, which will ultimately help preserve U.S. national security and international security as the climate changes in coming decades. Without this level of commitment and integration, the U.S. risks being caught off-guard by climate-related crises that may have grave regional and geopolitical consequences, like the conflict in Syria."*[10]

Whatever you may think about the impact the decision will have on the environment, America's national security will be adversely affected. The military has long thought of climate change as a "threat multiplier." A 2014 Defense Department report stated that *"rising global temperatures, changing precipitation patterns, climbing sea levels, and more extreme weather events will intensify the challenges of global instability, hunger, poverty, and conflict."*[11] Higher oceans menace 128 military bases and a 2016 report from the Union of Concerned Scientists found that the largest naval installation in the world, Naval Station Norfolk, will face increasing water levels of up to seven feet.[12]

Since the Trump Administration dropped climate change from the latest National Security Strategy's list of chief threats, many believe, including Anatol Lieven, writing in January 2018's edition of *Foreign Policy*, that it's time for the U.S. military to make its voice heard. Lieven argues persuasively that there are two key issues involved and that the U.S. military has a duty to "instruct" Americans on the threat caused by global warming.

> *"The first is that as an institution that depends on science for its weapons and intelligence systems, the US defense establishment not only has a keen understanding of its importance, but can remind the American public of the vital urgency of reckoning with scientific fact.*
>
> *"The second relates to the role of patriotism and nationalism in America. At present, climate change has been turned — quite unnecessarily — into an issue that divides Americans rather than unites them. Nationalism is the only force in the United States and elsewhere that can motivate the masses to make sacrifices in the struggle against climate change...* "[13]

Academics are not the only ones who have objected. On January 12, 2018, a bipartisan group of 106 House members sent a letter to the president asking him to reconsider the omission of climate change, quoting Defense Secretary James Mattis: "*The effects of climate... change will impact our security situation.*"[14]

Climate change is a scientific fact and ignoring it affects our national security.

HOAX?

By withdrawing from the Paris accord, Trump vowed to stand against what he called a "draconian" international deal. The only way his decision makes any sense is if global warming is indeed a hoax. Unfortunately, global warming is a reality. Over the last 150 years, burning fossil fuels has resulted in a 25% increase in the amount of carbon dioxide in our atmosphere. Since record keeping began in the late 1800s, the global average surface temperature has risen significantly. Air pollution in the form of green-house gases, like carbon dioxide, could seal in the earth's heat and significantly raise global surface temperatures over the next 50 years.[15]

Recent research has found that storm intensity and duration increase as global warming emissions increase in the atmosphere. Both the duration and intensity of hurricanes have doubled in recent decades, a trend that corresponds to increases in average ocean surface temperatures over the same period.[16] Rising sea levels, also caused in part by rising global temperatures, intensify storm damage. The warmer the ocean, the greater the potential for stronger storms, like Hurricanes Katrina, Harvey, and Irma, which cause massive property damage and loss of life. While the total number of storms during the last three decades has remained constant, the percentage of Category 4 and 5 hurricanes has increased considerably.[17]

Since the clean-up of hurricanes such as Andrew ($43.7 billion) and Katrina (upwards of $125 billion) is so costly, with Harvey expected to break all records, it's imperative that we take all necessary steps to minimize the damage caused by these storms. Studies project that the earth's average temperature will increase between 2.5 degrees and 10.4 degrees by 2100 if no major efforts are undertaken to reduce the emissions of greenhouse gases.[18] If temperatures rise as projected, the following is likely to occur:

- A rise in sea level between 3.5 and 34.6 inches. Each one-meter rise will cause the shoreline to retreat by nearly a mile.

- Severe stress on forests, wetlands, alpine regions, and other natural ecosystems.

- A greater threat to human health as mosquitos and other disease-carrying insects and rodents spread diseases over larger regions.

- A disruption of agriculture due to increased temperatures, water stress, and sea level.[19]

As reported in *Forbes* magazine on February 1, 2017, the U.S. emitted 5.4 billion tons of carbon dioxide in 2015, with a cost per ton of $36, which means that the U.S. is paying $200 billion to cover the costs of all the emissions being burned.[20] In other words, the fossil fuel industry is receiving a hidden $200 billion subsidy. This is an actual cost in lost labor productivity, healthcare costs, increased energy expenditures, and coastal damage that is paid somewhere in the world for each ton of carbon dioxide that is emitted.

Most Americans are not aware of such subsidies, nor do they seem to understand that with their hard-earned tax dollars they are subsidizing crop-withering heat waves, melting ice, rising seas, and more destructive storms.

While economic growth is often seen as the savior of all problems, the global economy is outgrowing the capacity of the earth to support it. In other words, we are consuming renewable resources faster than they can regenerate. Even though the U.S. has 1/20 of the world's population, it consumes one-quarter of the world's natural resources. China is now the leading consumer of basic commodities, replacing America in consumption of grain, meat, coal, and steel. If current trends continue, by 2031, China's grain consumption will take in 2/3 of the world's grain, its paper consumption will totally wipe out the world's forests and its oil consumption will reach 99 million barrels a day, a real problem since global oil production in 2016 was 97 million barrels and most experts think we've nearly reached the peak.[21] The inability of governments to manage the energy transition could lead to failed states and, for the U.S., a diminished role in world affairs.

One of the worst aspects of America's withdrawal from the Paris agreement was the terrible message it sent to the world. *"Just think of yourselves,"* it conveyed to a global audience, *"don't worry about the world as a whole or about future generations."* It was a selfish, irresponsible, and arrogant point of view. The issue here is not just carbon emissions, but rather sacrifices that a responsible society takes. Trump's attitude is "screw everybody else."

There are no simple answers. The security of our nation, the health of its economy, and our common future depend on the prudent management of our environment. If we are not to leave a devastated world to the next generation, our stewardship of the planet must transcend political party and short-term interests. We must work together with the other nations of the world. If we keep choosing short-term consumption over long-term environmental issues, we will commit our nation, and our planet, to increased political turmoil, pollution, conflict over resources, adverse climatic changes, and terrorism.

If we continue to tell the world to go screw itself, eventually the very underpinnings of human life will be threatened. The U.S. must end its dependence on foreign oil, increase energy efficiency, harness renewable energy sources and once again join the civilized world as a member of the Paris Agreement. The benefits will be a reduced balance of payments, less air pollution, increased jobs, a reduction in greenhouse gases, and less vulnerability to terrorists.

It is indisputable that the actions of humans are irreversibly harming the earth, which forces us to ask three questions. Why should we ignore God's command to be stewards of the earth? What gives us the right to tell the whole world that we're going to continue to harm the planet and there is nothing they can do about it? Lastly, how can we justify turning over to our children a world that is more polluted and harmed than we received it?

We have been blessed by God with a planet of incomparable beauty. To wastefully squander those precious resources and pollute our world is not only poor national policy, unscientific and unpatriotic, but immoral as well.

9

WORK

"*Give me six hours to chop down a tree and I will spend the first four sharpening the axe.*"
Abraham Lincoln

"*Come to me all of you who are weary and carry heavy burdens and I will give you rest.*"
Jesus, Matthew 11:28

"*Learn some and drink some and draw some and taint some and sing and dance and play and work every day some.*"
All I Really Need to Know I Learned in Kindergarten

NFL coaches are always searching for an edge over their opponent and in the age of computers, the analyzing has become more technical. A relatively new concept, many coaches now have assistants called the "Quality Control Coach." They don't actually coach, but spend all day multitasking, breaking down film, analyzing data, and even running the scout team in practice. When Mike Holmgren was the Offensive Coordinator for the San Francisco 49ers in 1990, he needed someone to transcribe the team playbook and copy it to a computer. That someone was Jon Gruden. The job also included analyzing opponents, breaking down statistics, tracking and charting plays during games, and getting coffee. Gruden earned $500 a month, worked 18 hour-days and often slept in the office. This job allowed him to pick up valuable seasoning and, ultimately, he became the head coach with Oakland and Tampa Bay and the winning coach of the 2003 Super Bowl.

Thirty years ago, no one had ever heard of a Quality Control Coach. Now, the QC job has become so important that even Special-Teams coordinators are asking for their own Quality-Control coaches, and QC coaches now have agents. That is how it is in America in 2018. Many jobs from the past no longer exist as the world and industries change. The answer to keeping America great is not to focus on bringing back coal mining jobs but to look to the future.

Although some in Washington want to pretend we live in a bubble unattached to the world, it is a global marketplace that we have to deal with. *"Here's what's going to happen,"* Trump said at a 2016 rally about the Indiana company, Carrier. *"They're going to call me, and they are going to say, 'Mr. President, Carrier has decided to stay in Indiana.'"* He kept going. *"One hundred percent,"* Trump said. *"It's not like we have an 80% chance of keeping them or a 95%. 100%."* After the election, Trump took credit for rescuing the Carrier jobs, tweeting on Thanksgiving that he had cut a deal with the company. Trump visited the factory in December and announced that, thanks to his negotiating, more than 1,100 of the jobs would stay in the heartland. *"Carrier stepped it up, and now they're keeping over 1,100 people,"* Trump told an audience of cheering factory workers.

However, Carrier informed the state of Indiana in July 2017 that it would soon begin cutting 632 workers from an Indianapolis factory and move the jobs to Monterrey, Mexico. Michael Strain, director of economic policy studies at the right-leaning American Enterprise Institute, said Trump's deal with Carrier offered a partial solution to a broader problem. American manufacturing employment, he noted, has dwindled for decades, especially in Indiana, where a third of workers held those jobs 50 years ago; the share today is closer to 10%.[1]

Leaving aside Trump's tendency to not be truthful, his problem on work is that he mistakenly believes that we can return to the 1950s and that the United States can prosper in isolation. He is wrong on both counts. Let's look at two areas where we can move America forward (infrastructure and renewable energy) and increase the number of workers.

INFRASTRUCTURE

Paving the nation's roads, building its canals, and utilizing its natural resources for commerce has been a pressing issue since the Washington Administration. Alexander Hamilton promoted debt-financed "internal improvements" for roads, canals, ports, and the like while Senator Henry Clay made his name in the early 1800s by promoting an aggressive "American system" of improvements. In the 1850s, the Republican Party was committed to infrastructure projects, especially the construction of the transcontinental railroad. President Roosevelt helped build the Hoover Dam and power the rise of the American Southwest. The modern pinnacle of government infrastructure was the building of the interstate highway system in the 1950s under Republican Dwight Eisenhower, which changed America forever.

In times of economic recession, putting people to work provides an important stimulus. The United States is no longer in a grinding recession, but President Trump was right to focus on infrastructure during the presidential campaign. The country had been spending about 20% less on water and transportation infrastructure than in 1959, while having to meet the demands of today's old and huge network of roads and sewers.[2] No one doubts that infrastructure repairs are urgently needed everywhere, in both red states and blue states. The question is: how do we do it?

Trump campaigned on spending one trillion dollars to fix the nation's infrastructure and, after much delay, he unveiled a plan in June 2017. However, Trump didn't want the federal government to spend a lot of money hiring people to pave roads and build bridges. Rather, his plan promoted tax cuts as a way to get private industry to pay for all repairs. In theory, there's nothing wrong with private investment in infrastructure and Speaker of the House Paul Ryan has stated that every $1 in targeted tax cuts can spur $40 of infrastructure spending. Many disagree. "*Private investment is important, but it's by no means sufficient,*" says Ed Rendell, the former mayor of Philadelphia and governor of Pennsylvania who co-chairs *Building America's Future*, a bipartisan group pushing for more infrastructure investments. "*Tax credits can only do so much. The lion's share has to come from the federal government. Don't screw around.*"[3]

As a share of the economy, federal infrastructure investment is about half of what it was thirty-five years ago.[4] Meanwhile, countries like China are racing ahead. Consumers pay more for everything from food to furniture because of freight congestion in our highways, waterways and ports. Our deteriorating roads result in a hidden "pothole tax," rush-hour commuters waste dozens of hours in traffic annually — costing them nearly $1,000 per year in fuel and other expenses, while a fifth of American flights are either delayed or cancelled.[5]

It is estimated that every $1 billion in infrastructure investment creates nearly 13,000 jobs and that every dollar of infrastructure investment will lead to a $1.60 increase in GDP the following year and twice that over the ensuring 20 years.[6]

We need to substantially increase federal infrastructure funding over the next several years. Infrastructure investment is a major down payment on a stronger America. We need to harness both public and private capital to fix and expand our bridges and roads, create more public transit options, improve our airports and aviation technology, improve our rail system, make sure that all Americans are connected to the Internet, improve the ability for businesses to connect with their customers and suppliers, improve our water and wastewater systems, and create a world-class energy infrastructure.

President Trump has said that he wants to see a bipartisan solution in 2018 to the infrastructure problem. I hope that comes to fruition. We must invest in America's future, but we need to make sure taxpayers are getting the most bang for their buck and that projects are selected on impact rather than politics.

RENEWABLE ENERGY JOBS

According to President Trump, we need to "bring back" certain jobs, like coal mining, and he promised that if elected, he would do so. However, the coal mining jobs that he promised are not coming back. The future is not in coal mining, but in renewable energy jobs. If the U.S. does not get on the bandwagon, the rest of the world will and we will fall way behind.

As prices fall and interest in clean power rises, renewable energy jobs are increasing all over the world. The United States has seen explosive growth in renewable energy jobs over the past three years, led by solar jobs (up 82%) and wind jobs (up 100%).[7] In 2016, solar jobs had risen to more than 260,000, a job creation rate 17 times the rate of the national economy.[8] The increase alone is more than twice the total number of coal mining jobs (51,000) in the United States today.[9] Moreover, jobs in the U.S. wind industry doubled from around 51,000 at the end of 2013 to over 102,000 at the end of 2016 and a new wind turbine went up every 2.4 hours in 2016.[10] According to the Department of Energy (DOE), over three million Americans were employed by the clean energy industry in Q1 2016.[11] According to a 2015 report from the Environmental Defense Fund, renewable energy jobs in the United States enjoyed a six percent compound annual growth rate between 2012 and 2015.[12] Fossil fuel jobs, by contrast, had a negative 4.5% compound annual growth rate over the same time period.[13]

The total number of U.S. renewable energy jobs still falls short of other countries, however. The U.S. trails the European Union, about 806,000 jobs to over 1.2 million. Brazil also has more renewable energy jobs, with 876,000. All three are far behind China, the world leader in clean energy employment with nearly 4 million jobs.[14] Worldwide, nearly ten million people are now employed in the renewable energy industry. Meanwhile, the Trump Administration is proposing deep cuts to investment in clean energy innovation in its 2018 budget. This makes little sense because not only are renewable energy jobs on the rise, employment in the coal industry has been falling in many countries. U.S. coal mining jobs have also been declining over the past 30 years, from 150,000 in 1987 to 51,000 in 2017.[15]

Trump seems to be blinded when it comes to energy, with his backward-looking focus on fossil fuels. The solar power sector employed twice as many workers in 2016 than power generation from coal, gas and oil combined.[16] Not only are solar jobs growing much faster than the rest of the U.S. economy, they are generating more jobs per dollar invested – more than double the jobs created from investing in fossil fuels. Jobs in renewables and energy efficiency are also growing. Wind and solar jobs increased by 32% and 25% respectively between 2015–2016, while coal-fired power generation in the U.S. declined by 53%, mainly because of cheap and cleaner natural gas, the share of which grew by 33% in that decade.[17] Fracking and newer drilling techniques have led to a surge in natural gas production so that supply now exceeds demand. The costs of solar and wind continue to plummet.

On many occasions, Trump has promised to make American coal great again.

By the end of 2016, the nation's mines only totaled one-seventh of what they were in the 1970s and there's little desire because of cheap natural gas to use more coal at home. With or without the Paris agreement, any return of America's coal production, coal-fired power plants, and mining jobs is a nearly impossible task.

"Coal plants have closed down and you're not reopening them," said Andrew Cosgrove, an energy analyst at Bloomberg Intelligence. *"Low natural gas prices, at the end of the day, have decimated most of the U.S. coal production."*[18]

In 2008, the U.S. produced a record 1.2 billion tons of coal which generated about half of U.S. electricity. Since then, due to cheap and cleaner-burning natural gas, U.S. power generators have drastically increased their use of gas and renewables. In 2017, according to the Energy Information Administration, coal generated just 30% of America's power.[19] Despite what Donald Trump says, coal is not coming back and renewables is a good business move.

CITIES AND STATES ON THEIR OWN

Despite little support from the federal government, several cities and states are pursuing policies to transition from fossil fuels to renewable energy. Massachusetts is considering a bill that would require the state to obtain *all* of its energy from renewable resources by 2050, as is California. Hawaii has already passed such a law. Altogether, two dozen American cities have committed to switching to renewable energy, with many pledges coming after the election.

The day before Trump's withdrawal of the U.S. from the Paris Climate Accord, State Senate Leader Kevin de León from Los Angeles said California should continue with its renewable energy goals not only to fight climate change, but because it makes economic sense.

"We have already seen the economic benefits of clean energy policies," De León said on the Senate floor on May 31, 2017. *"Today, California is home to over 100,000 solar jobs."* He made his comments as he promoted a plan to require California produce 100% of its energy from renewable sources by 2045. He also said, *"Clean energy is, in fact, a pillar of our economy that employs now more than half a million Californians. That's nearly ten times more the number of coal mining jobs that exist in the entire nation. So, clean energy is the future."*[20]

Investing in clean energy is the key for rebuilding our economy for the future. Not only will it create thousands of jobs, it will also increase energy independence and protect public health. Besides the obvious fact that renewable energy reduces greenhouse gas emissions and other harmful air pollutants, a worthy goal in itself, investments in clean energy produce many more jobs per dollar than gas, oil, or coal. Clean energy jobs and businesses have grown much faster than the economy as a whole in the past twenty years and continued to grow even during the economic downturn. We are in the midst of an Environmental Revolution, comparable to the Agricultural and Industrial Revolutions that preceded it. Restructuring the economy based on ecological principles perhaps represents the greatest investment opportunity in history. Despite what Donald Trump says, the era of fossil fuels is nearing an end and we must be prepared to make the transition to the new reality.

We must look forward, not backward, and focus on new industries, which will create new jobs and help us remain the world's strongest country. If we don't accept this challenge, the United States will be relegated to a second-tier nation. It's as simple as that.

SPECIAL TEAMS

10

RESPONSIBILITY (DEBT AND POVERTY)

"You cannot escape the responsibility of tomorrow by evading it today."
Abraham Lincoln

"'Now which of these three would you say was a neighbor to the man who was attacked by bandits?' Jesus asked. The man replied, 'The one who showed him mercy.' Then Jesus said, 'Yes, now go and do the same.'"
Jesus, Luke 10:36-37

"Share everything."
All I Really Need to Know I Learned in Kindergarten

After 56 years in San Diego, the San Diego Chargers announced on January 12, 2017 that they were moving to Los Angeles where, starting in 2019, they will share a $2.66 billion dollar stadium with the Los Angeles Rams. The lack of a modern stadium in San Diego and the additional revenues such stadiums generate prompted the team's departure. The decision to move came two months after San Diego voters rejected a ballot proposition for a combined stadium and convention center annex the Chargers proposed for downtown. NFL Commissioner Roger Goodell said that the team did everything it could to find a stadium solution. San Diego's mayor, however, disagreed and said the city had a reasonable stadium approach but that the Chargers wanted too much taxpayer money. City Councilman Chris Ward said it wouldn't have been appropriate for the city to spend taxpayer money to keep the team.

> *"The Chargers have not earned a place in line ahead of the thousands of hard working San Diegans who have supported them for decades," Ward said. "It is a sad day for fans that the Chargers commitment to our city was ultimately contingent on receiving hundreds of millions of tax payer dollars, but now we can finally move forward as a community."* [1]

So, my beloved San Diego Chargers – and the memories of Lance Alworth, Dan Fouts, Junior Seau, LaDanian Tomlinson, Phillip Rivers, and Antonio Gates, among many others – evaporated into history because of "tax payer" money. The team could have been saved if the city council was willing to stick the tax payers with a huge bill that would burden them and their children for generations. As much as I love football, I'm glad they chose the responsible way be cause the price was too high, a lesson that our nation's leaders have not yet mastered.

Although the national debt is now an eye-popping $21 trillion, neither candidate discussed it much in the 2016 election. And while Republicans have historically championed fiscal responsibility, they have thrown such positions to the wind. Shortly after reducing revenue through the tax cut of December 2017, President Trump signed a budget in March 2018 that will greatly increase spending, the combination of which will add at least two trillion dollars to the total debt as well as lead to annual trillion dollar deficits. But it's not just Republicans as Democrats have also ducked the tough decisions that need to be made. And so in one of the few areas where there is bipartisanship, members of both parties continue to bury their heads in the sand and hope that the day of reckoning doesn't come for a while.

While some might possibly escape, millions of young Americans will not. Over the next decade, we will spend around ***seven trillion dollars***-around $55,000.00 per household-simply to service the interest on the debt.[2] By 2030, every single dollar of the federal budget will go to entitlement programs like Social Security and Medicare and to interest. *There won't be any money left for anything else.* This is not my opinion or an ideological statement. *It's mathematical.* Deficits and debt are a form of child abuse. "We're ultimately mortgaging the future,"[3] says Romina Boccia, deputy director for economic policy at the Heritage Foundation.

While prior generations have striven to leave a stronger nation to those that follow, ours might be the first generation of Americans to leave our children and grandchildren, overwhelmed with debt, a weaker nation with fewer economic opportunities. The issues are complex and it is not enough to simply blame the other party. Success will take a bipartisan effort. But it's simply doing what is right. Every member of Congress should commit to not increasing the debt and if they are not willing to do so, they need to explain why our kids should pay our bills.

Our government has a responsibility to spend prudently, wisely, and not waste money. It also has a responsibility to make sure that its most underprivileged are not ignored for the flip side of responsibility is compassion. The United States, the greatest country in history, is great for many reasons, including its generosity and compassion. While a generalization, Republicans emphasize responsibility while Democrats focus on fairness and compassion. But both are important and are not mutually exclusive. We will never thrive as a nation if we remain locked in eternal battle with our blue or red opponent. So, with the goal of creating a government that works, let's look closer at these critical concepts.

DEBT

While deficits, debt, entitlements, consumption and investments involve many complex matters, the real issues are freedom and our future. Budgets are not just numbers; they are moral documents. As Jim Wallis says, they show what we care about.

From 1789 to 1959, our nation had mostly budget surpluses except during times of war and depression. Thomas Jefferson said that debt and revolution follow each other as cause and effect and *"the earth belongs to the generation alive at any given time. If one generation leaves its debt to encumber the next, then the earth should belong to the dead and not the living generation."* After almost thirty straight years of deficits, beginning in 1969, the United States had four surpluses in a row at the end of the 1990s, giving us a tremendous opportunity to pay down the debt. However, as of 2018, the debt is a mind-blowing $21 trillion.

To balance the books, the Treasury prints up new bonds, notes, and bills, and auctions them off every three months to investors willing to lend to Uncle Sam. China, Japan, Great Britain, and Caribbean banks have lent the U.S. trillions of dollars. By lending their money to us, they are financing our deficits, just like an automobile company finances the purchase of a new car. Unlike the automobile purchaser, the government doesn't have to pay down these loans. When it comes time to pay an investor, when a bond matures, the government just rolls over the loan by auctioning off more paper to another lender, using the money to pay back the loan that just matured. Every time Congress wants to spend more, it raises its limit.

As Peter Peterson, former Commerce Secretary for Richard Nixon and President of the Concord Coalition, a bipartisan, grass-roots organization dedicated to fiscal responsibility, often said, when the government borrows by selling government debt, it reduces the savings available for private investment. We pay for our deficits and consumption today by reducing society's well-being tomorrow. *Future American adults will be poorer so that today's American adults can live better.*[4] Read the previous sentence again and ask yourself if that bothers you.

While today's huge debt is bad for all of us, it will affect young people much greater than older people. In 2008, the first baby boomer retired and in 2039, the youngest will retire. If boomers insist on every benefit and tax cut for themselves, they will essentially be declaring war on our children. A single male who retired in 1965 received Social Security benefits worth an 8.5% return on the payroll taxes he paid into the system. A single male who retires in 2030 will get a return of 1%.[5] If payroll taxes are raised to make sure boomers get all their benefits, my kids and yours will get back less than what they paid in.

After decades of surpluses, Social Security now pays out more than it takes in. In the coming years, there will be more elderly people than before collecting benefits but far fewer workers taking their place and paying taxes into the system. Life expectancy has increased from 45 in 1900 to 78.7 as of 2010 and the elderly will more than double in the years to come. In 2006 there were about 88,000 centenarians. By 2050, there will be over a million.[6] This is not speculation; it's a mathematical certainty.

Moreover, Americans have been retiring earlier. In 1950, the average age of retirement was 68; today, it is 63 and dropping. Moreover, there will be a dramatic decrease in the rate of the U.S. population growth, even though the total population will continue to grow, reaching 400 million by 2043. The U.S. fertility rate in 1960 was 3 per woman; it was 1.84 as of 2015; 2.1 is the rate needed to maintain the status quo.[7] Consequently, we will either have to undertake a fundamental reform of senior benefits or have a fiscal meltdown. The only other way to pay for all this is to borrow from future generations, which is what we have been doing. Both parties are responsible. While Democrats say we can't budge on spending, Republicans say the same on taxes and so the gap keeps getting wider and the polarization increases. So, nobody does anything except blame others and the problem gets worse.

UNSUSTAINABLE

In 1994, the Bipartisan Commission on Entitlement and Tax Reform produced a report concluding that "current trends are not sustainable." Nearly 25 years later, nothing much has changed as federal budget policy remains on an unsustainable track. The thing about something that is unsustainable is that it is, well, unsustainable. For a while, things improved, resulting in budget surpluses in the late nineties. However, this short-lived trend ended in 2002 when tax cuts, military spending, and a mild recession plunged the budget into deficits again. Policy decisions and a much deeper recession led to even worse deficits and in 2009, the U.S. had its first annual trillion-dollar deficit.

As the economy recovered, spending decreased, tax revenues rose, and the deficit fell. However, deficits are on the rise again and trillion dollar deficits have returned. This time will be more challenging than before because nothing has been done to change the structural mismatch between spending and federal revenues.

Since entitlements are fixed by statute, under current law the debt is projected to reach an unprecedented 150% of GDP within 30 years.[8] This could actually be made worse by unexpected things such as future military engagements, recessions, or other national emergencies that would require additional borrowing.

When the federal government increases its borrowing, it competes with the private sector for available capital. This drains the savings we need to invest in the economy, slows workers' productivity, and reduces long-term growth. Furthermore, the larger the national debt is, the more we'll have to pay for interest payments. This is throwing money down the toilet since it's money that can't be spent on general services, national security, investments in the country's future, or to lower taxes. It's billions of dollars being spent solely to cover past borrowing.

To make fiscal policy sustainable, policymakers must adjust federal budgets to stabilize the national debt as a percentage of GDP and then put it on a downward trajectory. The Trump Administration has told us that the problem can be solved simply through growth. It cannot.

Unless changes are made, the status quo is unsustainable, and that never turns out well.

UNIVERSAL ENTITLEMENTS

Many have criticized those who receive food stamps and the like and claim the moral high ground. However, *all* groups receive some type of federal benefits, not just the poor. According to Peterson, Social Security benefits persuade people to retire earlier, farm aid leads to unproductive cultivation, and cost-plus Medicare reimbursement invites hospitals and doctors to over-treat, over-prescribe, and over-bill. Our tax code encourages people to take out larger mortgages and accept more expensive health insurance policies from their employers. "*Entitlements cost a lot today and will cost more tomorrow. They favor the rich over the poor, the old over the young, and consumption over savings. They dump random windfalls on those who don't need them and pass over those who do*," Peterson warned and as a result we have ended up with the ultimate paradox: *universal entitlements.*[9] Apparently, we are all victims and all deserve to be on welfare. In 2013, 69.4% of federal spending went to dependence-creating programs, up dramatically from 21.2% in 1962.[10]

We can demand that our leaders undertake long-term entitlement reforms that are needed to put the budget on a sustainable trajectory and face up to the required sacrifice. Alternatively, we can continue to pretend that our choices have no consequences and let our children pay the price in lost opportunities, lower living standards, and a less safe and secure place in the world. We're enslaving our kids and grandkids with policies that focus on ourselves at the expense of future generations. It is wrong. According to German theologian Dietrich Bonhoeffer, the ultimate test of a moral society is the kind of world it leaves to its children. Our government is failing this test miserably.

POVERTY

More than 45 million people, or nearly 15% of all Americans, lived in poverty in 2014 according to the Census Bureau.[11] Perhaps you are not included in this sobering statistic but poverty in the richest nation on earth is a shameful moral failure.

We live in the greatest, freest, and richest nation on earth and yet there are *millions* of people who don't have enough to eat and who don't have a place to sleep. That should shame every American, and especially every Christian, to the core. Many Christians forget that there are several thousand passages in the Bible about the poor. In the New Testament, one of every sixteen verses is about the poor or money. When you fall asleep tonight in your warm, comfortable bed, remember that people near you are diving through dumpsters looking for food and are defecating in the street.

It is said that everyone gets the same amount of ice during their lives. The difference, however, is that the rich get their ice in the summer while the poor get their ice in the winter. Victims of Hurricane Harvey were from every class of society, from the rich to the poor and in-between. The rain falls on everyone but the impact of the rain differs based on the size of your bank account. If the affluent lose their home, it's a few months of inconvenience from staying in hotels but ultimately, they will get their insurance check and possibly live in a newer and bigger home. The poor often lose everything they have with no chance of recoupment.

In 2016, more than 45 million people lived in poverty in the U.S. *Never* have so many Americans lived so poorly. If every person in the United States that is living in poverty lived in the same state, it would be the most populous state in the nation – the state of Poverty, USA. In the richest nation in the world, this should shock us.

NEVER-ENDING CYCLE

One of the most crippling effects of being poor is that it almost always insures an inferior education, which in turn nearly guarantees that the poverty will continue and be passed on to the next generation, creating a continuous cycle. Outraged, Democrats will castigate Republicans for abandoning the poor while the GOP will scream that Democratic policies have failed.

Conservatives argue that poverty is caused by the breakdown of the family, increased sex and violence on television, teen pregnancy, etc. Since America is the land of opportunity, where anyone can succeed with hard work, the argument goes, poor people have no one to blame but themselves. On the other hand, liberals claim that poverty can only be explained by looking at issues such as nutrition, housing, jobs, healthcare, etc. Although both are partially correct, both the right and left should be able to agree that it is deplorable that millions of Americans go to bed hungry and have nowhere to sleep.

As Jim Wallis points out, conservatives will argue that the solution is to strengthen the family and they are right. Clearly, bad personal and moral choices often 'result in people ending up in unenviable positions, while marriage is the best anti-poverty measure that exists. Liberals will speak passionately of structural inequities and they too are right, for family values will not guarantee that you will receive a fair wage or health insurance. There is a deep chasm between those who believe that more compassionate policies will solve the problem and those who attribute everything to the breakdown of the family and sexual immorality.

Why can't we develop and fund programs that assist the needy while promoting policies that encourage strong families and values? Overcoming poverty should be a bipartisan commitment, one that, as Wallis states, should link religious values with economic justice and moral behavior with political commitment. A society should be judged not by its wealth and power but by how it treats its most vulnerable members.

OUR OWN BEST INTERESTS

Moral reasons aside, there are actually strong economic reasons for not abandoning the poor and working towards a "100%" America. Many economists, as well as the Congressional Budget Office, have concluded that economic growth will be stronger and more sustainable if all Americans, and not just certain segments, contribute economically and participate fully in modern society. While is it sad that millions are not fulfilling the American dream, it has negative effects on those who are. If people are not inclined to help those less fortunate for moral reasons, they should do so for their own selfish reasons.

Many wealthy people put the blame on the poor themselves, rationalizing that they must deserve their lot in life because they are weak, stupid, and lazy. They argue that if you work hard, you should not be poor. This perspective, whatever merit it might have theoretically, does not solve the problem that there are nearly 50 million Americans living in poverty. Don't help them because you care for them or love them, but instead help them because doing so will help you. Millions of people in poverty do not help this country but a rising tide lifts all boats.

Scotsman Adam Smith, the patron saint of American capitalism, argued that instinctive self-interest would, in the framework of the marketplace, create a self-regulating economic order. Smith, however, did not believe in unfettered markets, as he realized that human envy would destroy the empathy necessary for a successful market. In today's America, a period of unprecedented affluence and prosperity, we have great difficulty in setting limits to our materialistic cravings. The balance that Smith so eloquently wrote of between individual desire and social responsibility has become increasingly threatened. Not only will it be impossible to sustain an unfettered global market with no limits, it is immoral to even try. The more one accumulates, the less there is for others. Rabid consumption, therefore, is not only counterproductive, it is selfish and runs counter to Smith's philosophies.

The American dream has become an illusion that all can become wealthy, since the gap between rich and poor has widened. So, Adam Smith's vision of an evolved market, where the ingenuity of self-interest finds balance with the benevolence to the social benefit of all, is sadly unrealized.

POVERTY AFFECTS US ALL

Poverty breeds poverty. As Billie Holiday once sang: "*Them that's got shall get, them that's not shall lose. So the Bible says, and it still is news.*" Many people think that poverty doesn't affect them, but the general population pays a heavy price for allowing poverty to exist. The following report from the Children's Defense Fund leaves no doubt:

> "*When children do not succeed as adults, all of society pays the price. Businesses are able to find fewer good workers, consumers pay more for their goods, hospitals and health insurers spend more treating preventable illnesses, teachers spend more time on remediation and special education, private citizens feel less safe*

on the streets, governors hire more prison guards, mayors must pay to shelter homeless families, judges must hear more criminal, domestic, and other cases, taxpayers pay for problems that could have been prevented, fire, and medical workers must respond to emergencies that never should have happened, and funeral directors must bury children who never should have died." [12]

We must work vigorously to combat poverty, not only because it is the right thing to do, but because it will benefit all of society, and each of us, if we do. It is at the same time in our best interests to do so and shameful to not do so. As the old proverb says, *"Poverty is no shame for those who have not. Poverty is a shame for those who have. A poor man shames us all."*

Seeing people living in the streets and eating out of dumpsters should enrage us. We should passionately demand that individuals, the church and the government do more. We need to be like the abolitionists who vigorously fought to end slavery before the Civil War. William Lloyd Garrison wrote the following about eradicating slavery and I suggest his attitude be applied to talking to others about freeing themselves from poverty and debt.

"I will be as harsh as truth and as uncompromising as justice. On this subject, I do not wish to think, or speak or write, with moderation. No! No! Tell a man whose house is on fire to give a moderate alarm; tell him to moderately rescue his wife from the hands of the ravisher; tell the mother to gradually extricate her babe from the fire into which it has fallen; but urge me not to use moderation in a cause like the present. I am in earnest — I will not equivocate, I will not excuse, I will not retreat a single inch, and I will be heard." [13]

Trump promised that he will fight for the forgotten man. Will those people be remembered? Will their voice be heard? Will anyone care?

"CHRISTMAS GIFT FOR THE MIDDLE CLASS"

In late December 2017, without a single Democratic vote, Congress passed a tax cut bill which President Trump signed into law, declaring the "biggest cuts in history" to be a Christmas gift for the middle class that would not add to the deficit. All three of those statements are false. As usual, Trump exaggerated as the cuts were not even close to being the biggest ever. Second, the legislation was heavily skewed towards the wealthy. Lastly, it will add up to two trillion dollars to the national debt. It used to be that Republicans were concerned about running up the debt and the deficit but in the Trump era, that train is long gone.

First, let's look at the many exaggerations in the president's proclamations.

On numerous occasions, Trump has said, "*It's the largest tax cut in the history of our country.*" Despite his penchant for repeating false things over and over as if the repetition will make something true, Trump has simply refused to recognize larger tax cuts in history, of which there have many. An October analysis by the Committee for a Responsible Federal Budget found that it would be the eighth biggest since 1918.[14] While the tax bill is certainly a large reduction, Trump constantly loses credibility with nearly non-stop exaggeration.

The president has repeatedly asserted that "it's a tax bill for the middle class," but average people are not the prime beneficiaries of the tax cuts. The nonpartisan Tax Policy Center estimates the biggest benefit of the new law will go to households making $308,000 to $733,000 who will receive a tax cut worth 3.4% of their after-tax income while middle-income earners will receive about 1.6%, the center estimates.[15] Moreover, only high-income people would get a meaningful tax cut after 2025, when nearly all of the plan's individual income tax provisions are due to expire.[16]

Trump has also declared that "Obamacare has been repealed in this bill" despite the fact that it hasn't, although the tax plan does end the individual mandate, which fines for people who don't carry health insurance. Other key components of Obamacare remain, such as the Medicaid expansion serving low-income adults, protections regarding people with pre-existing medical conditions, income-based subsidies for consumers buying individual health insurance policies, the requirement that insurers cover "essential" health benefits, and the mandate that larger employers provide coverage to their workers or face fines, to name a few.

Trump has also exaggerated the subject of future growth. *"So, we're at 3.3% GDP. I see no reason why we don't go to 4%, 5%, and even 6%,"* Trump speculated at a Cabinet meeting. However, there are no signs the economy is capable of delivering such a phenomenal growth rate and most mainstream economists expect economic growth to be closer to 2%. To generate growth of 6%, the cuts would have to spur over a trillion dollar gain to the GDP. Nothing has established how that would be remotely possible.

Secondly, the tax bill was slanted in favor of the wealthy and will greatly benefit corporations and "pass-through" businesses that advantage owners of companies with highly valued assets but few actual employees. Nearly all of the more than 500 private businesses Trump has claimed on his financial disclosure documents — including his umbrella company, the Trump Organization — are pass-throughs, so the bulk of his income will likely see an immediate tax break. Tax experts said real estate, rental, and leasing businesses will benefit more than any other industry. That change alone could save Trump millions. The new plan will also reduce the estate tax, which affects the inheritances of a few thousand of America's wealthiest families, including Trump's. The tax bill will allow a married couple to pass on up to $22 million in assets without having to pay the tax.

The biggest chunk of the plan offers a large and permanent tax cut for American companies, dropping the corporate rate from 35% to 21%. Income tax rates for everyone will drop temporarily, though the financial impact will be concentrated at the top. Families earning less than $25,000 a year would receive an average tax cut of $60; families making between $50,000 and $75,000 will get an average cut of $890; and families making more than $1 million would get an average cut of nearly $70,000, according to the nonpartisan Tax Policy Center.[17]

By 2027, 53% of Americans would pay more in taxes under the tax bill the Tax Policy Center stated.[18] That year, 82.8% of the bill's benefit would go to the top 1%.[19] Even in the first years of the bill's implementation, when it's an across-the-board tax cut, the benefits of the law would be heavily concentrated among the upper-middle and upper-class Americans, with nearly two-thirds of the benefit going to the richest fifth of Americans in 2018. Moreover, the repeal of the individual mandate could cause as many as 13 million fewer people to have health insurance, reducing federal spending for poor and middle-class Americans' health insurance by $338 billion over ten years, according to the CBO.[20] That worsens the bill's distribution for the poor and middle-class. Almost all provisions of the bill, with the exception of the reduction in the corporate tax rate from 35% to 21%, are temporary, expiring at the end of 2025.[21]

The rich and ultra-rich, by contrast, would continue to see massive tax breaks due to the corporate provisions. The top 1% would receive an average cut of $20,660. The top 0.1%, the richest of the rich earning $5.1 million or more a year, would get $148,260 back on average.[22] According to CBS News, Trump told a group of wealthy guests a few days before Christmas at a dinner at Mar-a-Lago, where initiation fees cost $200,000, "*You all just got a lot richer*," which makes it harder to believe it's a middle-class tax cut. By contrast, nearly 70% of Americans in the middle fifth of the income distribution — earning $54,700 to $93,200 a year in 2017 dollars — would see their taxes go up.[23] Republicans in support of the bill have, naturally, focused less on 2027, when much of the bill's changes will have expired, than on 2018 through 2025, when all its cuts, including for individuals, will be in effect. They hope that they can brag about "relief" experienced by most people and hope that people are too stupid to realize that most would end up paying more later down the road.

Third, the tax bill is fiscally irresponsible and because it adds up to two trillion dollars to the backs of our kids and grandkids, it's immoral. According to the Concord Coalition, a non-partisan group that focuses on fiscally responsibility, the bill is *"based on flawed economics, poor tax policy, and a troubling legislative process that has allowed little time for careful analysis."*[24] Concord's Executive Director Robert L. Bixby says that *"Its disingenuous combination of gimmicks and debt will not deliver the promised economic benefits, and the rushed, secretive process that produced this plan, with its many special-interest provisions, is bound to produce unwelcome surprises."*[25] As a result of this bill, the federal debt, which is already quite high by historical standards, is projected to increase by up to two trillion dollars over the already projected 10 trillion over the next decade.[26] Moreover, gimmicks in the bill, such as "sunsets" never intended to take effect, hide its true cost, meaning that the debt will probably be even higher. The revenue loss would come just as the healthcare and retirement costs of retiring baby boomers are adding to the already astronomical debt, which will be made even worse when lawmakers will most likely increase spending on defense, border security, and disaster relief.

Moreover, while tax cuts can be beneficial under certain circumstances, none is present here. *"The economy does not currently need fiscal stimulus,"* Bixby has said. *"Unemployment is low, corporate profits are high, and the Federal Reserve is raising interest rates."* Most importantly, the argument that tax cuts will pay for themselves with massive growth is fantasy. *"Tax cuts don't pay for themselves — even with generous assumptions about their possible impact on economic growth,"* Bixby said categorically. *"Eventually there will need to be tax increases or spending cuts to pay for this legislation.*

The bill leaves unanswered how that would be done, who would pay, and how that would affect the economy." [27]

Although there is no economically sound justification for a tax cut at this time, we are taking this cut and asking that someone else (our kids and grandkids) pay for it. Please ask yourself if you are OK with this.

We cannot just ignore millions of people living in poverty by pretending that they don't count and we cannot place our kids and grandkids into poverty by escalating a debt that we don't want to pay. Responsible people don't ask their kids to pay their debts. Such policies are, and there is no other way to say this, un-American, ungodly, and immoral.

PART THREE

A TEAM FOR THE AGES

11

WILL IT BENEFIT ALL? (OR JUST ME?)

"Don't worry when you are not recognized, but strive to be worthy of recognition."
Abraham Lincoln

"If you love only those who love you, what reward is there for that? Even corrupt tax collectors do that much."
Jesus, Matthew 5:46

"Remember the little seed in the Styrofoam cup: the roots go down and the plant goes up and nobody really knows how or why but we are all like that."
All I Really Need to Know I Learned in Kindergarten

The first NFL All-Star Game was played in 1939 in Los Angeles. The site of the game was moved around a lot before the game was moved to Aloha Stadium in Hawaii for 30 straight seasons. After leaving Hawaii for a while, the game returned there in 2016. Players are voted into the

Pro Bowl by the coaches, the players themselves, and the fans, although players whose teams advance to the Super Bowl do not play in the Pro Bowl.

Selection is an honor but the game is constantly criticized since the players do not give a 100% effort. It's mostly a vacation and many go through the motions during the game, thinking about getting to the pool. It's interesting that while the game is being played, on the weekend between the Conference Championship games and the Super Bowl, the members of the two Super Bowl teams, many of whom are not all-stars, are giving it their absolute best to get ready for the big game. The reason for that is simple: Football is a team game, not an individual game.

IS PASTEL A COLOR?

Most Republicans are principled people and most Democrats are honorable. However, whatever side you align with, realize that roughly half the country sees the world differently. The answer, therefore, is either constant conflict or principled resolutions achieved through negotiation and reasonable compromises. In other words, by seeking common ground.

Many on the far right or the far left despise the center, saying that it stands for nothing and that pastel is not a color. According to former Republican Senator John Danforth in his book *Faith and Politics*, partisan activists *"accomplish nothing and can accomplish nothing. They are all talk and no do. They have led us into stalemate."*[1] While you may believe that the opposing viewpoint is wrong, a stalemate will not help our kids. Some say that, by definition, moderates lack the passionate intensity of "true believers." If that is true, what would motivate a moderate to be active in politics? Danforth's answer is the same as mine: love of country and love of God. Specifically, he said:

> *"It is patriotism, the love of country more than self. It is a conviction that we will succeed in building the America and*

the world we want for our grandchildren only if we start by overcoming our differences and finding our common ground." [2]

That is the goal of this book, to find common ground so that all Americans can participate in this great experiment. The United States cannot be considered great unless it maximizes the potential for every single American, because as Alan Wolfe writes in his book *Return to Greatness*, *"No nation can be strong when, due to no fault of their own, such a high number of its citizens are rendered weak."* [3] Regardless of our political party or religious affiliation, we have no choice but to pursue national greatness. We owe it to our kids to make the world a better place for them.

Since both parties are capable of winning any election, the goal for the last several decades has been to get the base inflamed, engaged, and united. This strategy, however, has locked the country into a cultural war, which became especially obvious during the 2016 election. As explained by Stanley Greenberg in *The Two Americas*, each party works to excite the passions of its loyalists, creating additional partisanship. Consequently, America has become more polarized. If things are not going well, Trump will send out a controversial tweet about, say, transgender people, rallying his base, and that will take the attention off of something else. The problem with this approach is that, over time, it will destroy everything in its path.

Cultural politics has become, Greenberg points out, for all intents and purposes, a war, where *"there are few incentives for the warriors to relax, lest the other side gain an advantage."* [4] In the end, it becomes an exercise in futility, for neither side's base is big enough to guarantee a win. So, both sides focus on the groups that are most loyal by pouring gasoline on the fire through emotional wedge issues.

How do we become less polarized? There are no easy answers, but working towards a society where all people participate and benefit is not a Democrat or Republican issue. We should strive towards that goal because it is in our own best interests.

How do we get past this divide? The answer is to focus on the things that we can agree upon and use moral principles and the political common good as the capstones. Many emphasize that religion is personal and private, but, as Jim Wallis points out, restricting God to private space was the big flaw with 20th century evangelism. "*Exclusively private faith degenerates into a narrow religion, excessively preoccupied with individual and sexual morality while almost oblivious to the Biblical demands for public justice. In the end, private faith becomes a merely cultural religion providing the assurance of righteousness for people just like me.*"[5]

"*People just like me.*" That's how we make human suffering less real and more abstract. Sure, those people who suffered from Hurricane Katrina deserve help but *they're not like me*. It's really a shame about the homeless but *they're not like me*. So, the debate about issues like poverty becomes ideological and partisan.

It may be that only spirituality can bridge the two divides. The fundamental principle of separation of church and state does not require banishing moral and religious values from the public square. Such values shape our politics and our nation's social fabric. Progressives tend to ignore religion, but the failure to appreciate a basic element of public order alienates much of American society. On the other hand, conservatives assume that if *Roe v. Wade* is overturned and prayer is legally permitted in public schools, the nation will flourish. A moral society must be based upon more than simply enforcing the law. There has to be consent, which legislation on its own cannot accomplish.

A UNIFYING FORCE

Since many Americans believe in different faiths and think differently about what God expects of us, some would say that following "one nation under God" is a recipe for disaster. That being said, I believe Benjamin Franklin had it right when he said that the "*most acceptable service of God is doing good to man.*"[6]

Throughout different periods in history, governments have claimed that God was on their side. However, we should, as Lincoln said, worry about whether we are on God's side. Many on the right have placed the focus of religion in politics on sexual and cultural issues, such as abortion and gay rights, while ignoring weightier matters of justice. On the other hand, many on the left have fought for equality and justice from a completely secular point of view. Whatever your faith, religion has played a fundamental role in our nation's history and will continue to be a critical factor in our future. While there are dangers to blind adherence to religious dogma, religious or moral principles can be a unifying force that can bind this nation together.

Religion has been an instrumental factor in our country's history from the beginning. During the Constitutional Convention in 1787, the debate between small states and large states evolved into a hopeless deadlock as tempers flared and delegates threatened to walk out. Eighty-two-year-old Benjamin Franklin proposed a three day adjournment to let tempers cool and suggested the hiring of a chaplain who would "*introduce the business of each day by an address to the Creator of the Universe… beseeching Him to preside in our council, enlighten our minds with a portion of heavenly wisdom… and crown our labors with complete and abundant success.*"[7] The delegates did not walk out and, soon after, the Constitution was born.

Even though every president from George Washington to Donald Trump has mentioned God in his inauguration speech, religion can be a divisive force and can have negative consequences. Certainly, though, we can agree that as a nation we should pursue goals based on morality. Reinhold Niebuhr, in his book *Moral Man and Immoral Society*, wrote, "*A country will have authority and influence because of moral factors, not its military strength… and a nation without morality will soon lose its influence around the world."*[8]

In 1952, the U.S. Supreme Court stated in a precedent-setting decision, *"We are a religious people, whose institutions presuppose a Supreme Being."*[9] More than half a century later, the same can be said about today's citizenry, so let that be our starting point.

Many people use certain "wedge" issues that energize the "base" by pitting people of faith against their enemies, making civil discourse, much less compromise, nearly impossible. As former Republican Senator and minister John Danforth wrote in *Faith and Politics*, we must decide more than whether we are liberal or conservative, Democrat or Republican. We have to decide whether we want to be divisive or a reconciling force. While religion is a divisive force in our political system, Danforth forcefully says that religion must emphasize reconciliation.

Danforth attacks the practice of certain Catholic bishops who state publicly that Catholic candidates who support abortion are not welcome to receive communion, even though he is strongly pro-life. The former senator vigorously opposes this kind of certainty that creates a division between people who are on God's side and people who oppose God. Instead, he argues, we must strive for reconciliation that *"depends on acknowledging that God's truth is greater than our own,"* that we cannot reduce it to any political platform we create, no matter how committed we are to that platform, and that God's truth is large enough to accommodate the opinions of all kinds of people, even those with whom we strongly disagree.[10]

Many people believe that their religion knows God's will and that it can be translated into public policy. However, faith is not politics, as Danforth points out, for the real world in which government operates is comprised of both sinners and saints and no political agenda that humans create can justify a claim that it represents God's will.[11]

For more than a thousand years before the Declaration of Independence was drafted, the official state religion was that of the sovereign. James Madison and his cohorts came up with the novel concept that if the people of the United States were to be sovereign, and they belonged to a variety of different religions, the state religion would be no religion at all. Their emphasis was on "public religion," rather than on its private aspects, and so they spoke of God in a way that was unifying rather than divisive. The Declaration is a prime example:

- "When in the course of human events it becomes necessary for one people to dissolve the political bands which have connected them with another, and to assume among the powers of the earth, the separate and equal station to which the Laws of Nature and *Nature's God* entitles them…"

- "We hold these truths to be self-evident, that all men are created equal. That they are endowed by their *Creator*, with certain inalienable rights…"

- "We, therefore, the Representatives of the United States of America, in General Congress Assembled, appealing to the *Supreme Judge of the World*…"

- "And for the support of this Declaration, with a firm reliance on the protection of *Divine Providence*, we mutually pledge to each other our lives, our Fortunes and our sacred Honor."

The reverse side of the nation's seal (the image to the left on the back of the dollar bill) depicts the "Eye of Providence" above an unfinished pyramid with the words of the country's second motto: *Annuit Coeptis* – "God [or Providence] has favored our undertakings." While we cannot presume that God will favor our undertakings, we should strive to enact policies based on moral principles that bind us together and which God would favor.

FREE-RANGE CHICKEN

We cannot be a great nation nor bequeath a great legacy to the next generation if we ignore the plight of others who are different than us. We must work on making our country a 100% America.

On July 26, 2017, Trump stunned the world in a tweet that transgender members of the military would no longer be welcome, reversing a policy that had been put into effect by the Obama Administration. As a result of the swirling confusion caused by the apparently impulsive tweet, Gen. Joseph F. Dunford Jr., chairman of the Joint Chiefs, announced there would be "no modification" to current policy until the Pentagon received an actual directive from the president and the Defense Secretary to implement it. The Pentagon said in no uncertain terms that not even the president can change national policy simply by sending a tweet. On October 30, 2017, a federal court judge in Washington blocked the proposed ban and stated that the policy "does not appear to be supported by any facts."

Since no apparent thought went into this announcement, it seemed obvious that Trump was playing to his political base. Reaction from all quarters was swift and harsh, starting with the LGBT community and transgender members of the military, extending to Democratic and Republican lawmakers, to the public at large and ultimately to the Courts.

Senator John McCain said as follows:

> *"Any American who meets current medical and readiness standards should be allowed to continue serving. There is no reason to force service members who are able to fight, train, and deploy to leave the military — regardless of their gender identity... We should all be guided by the principle that any American who wants to serve our country and is able to meet the*

standards should have the opportunity to do so — and should be treated as the patriots they are." [12]

After months of legislative defeats and non-stop chaos, Trump stunned the political world by siding with the Democrats against his own party in September 2017 in connection with Hurricane Harvey relief and the debt ceiling. A week later came a supposed "deal" on DACA, which later unraveled. While I have been pushing bi-partisanship, it quickly became obvious that Trump's actions were not guided by principle or a reasoned attempt at compromise but were simply impulsive transactional attempts at upsetting the playing field. Who knows what he'll do or say tomorrow? Republicans were shell-shocked and Democrats were wary. Similar meetings, including a surreal one on guns after Parkland, have occurred since. How can any plans be made, how can goals be set, how can policy be constructed if there are no rules and it's just a mad scramble every day, untethered to any kind of philosophy?

Because of Trump's uncertain political loyalties and conflicting philosophical underpinnings, Washington has no idea what new alliance or policy U-turn might come next. Not only has the president been unwilling or unable to bring the warring factions of his party together, he has repeatedly attacked Republicans that he does not think are committed to his causes. His former Chief Strategist, Steve Bannon, made it known shortly after his departure from the White House in August of 2017 that he was "declaring war" on the GOP. Because of the uncertainty, many started speculating that the Republican party had reached a breaking point and would soon splinter and spawn a third party, although such thoughts partially died down after Bannon's Roy Moore loss and his release from Breitbart in January 2018.

"He's a free-range chicken," said Michael Steele, a former chairman of the Republican National Committee. *"And he's out there on the range playing with whomever he wants."* [13]

After Trump's movements toward the Democrats in September 2017, a number of pro-Trump supporters blasted him. *"Trump base is blown up, destroyed, irreparable, and disillusioned beyond repair,"* Rep. Steven King from Iowa said. Firebrand Ann Coulter tweeted *"At this point, who doesn't want Trump impeached?"* and *Breitbart News* ran a headline *"AMNESTY DON"* after the supposed agreement on DACA.[14] I don't think these right wingers totally understand the Trump base. While they definitely lean towards certain positions and policies, their support of Trump is not based on substantive issues; it's based on Trump. It's a cult of personality. When he said during the campaign that he could shoot somebody on Fifth Avenue, he wasn't joking. His hardcore supporters believe in him and support him no matter what. On November 20, 2017, an avid Trump supporter appeared on CNN's "New Day." When asked by host Alisyn Camerota about the alleged collusion with the Russians, Florida businessman Mark Lee said: *"Let me tell you. If Jesus Christ got down off the cross and told me Trump is with Russia, I would tell him, 'Hold on a second. I need to check with the president if it's true.'"*[15] This unwavering support is unprecedented and scary, but having one-third of Americans worshiping our president, one-third completely indifferent, and one-third despising him is not a formula for political or legislative success.

IS IT RIGHT?

As Lincoln so eloquently said, all people have been stamped with God's image and all people count because God doesn't make junk. Just as all of us should strive to treat others well, our government should strive to treat all citizens well. Oftentimes candidates ask the voters, *"Are you better off than you were four years ago?"* The better questions are these: 1) Is society as a whole more just? 2) Are all segments of the nation treated more or less fairly? 3) Is it right? These are the questions that we, as individual citizens, and we, as a government, should be asking. Martin Luther King put it this way:

"On some positions, cowardice asks the question, is it expedient? And then expedience comes along and asks the question, is it politic? Vanity asks the question, is it popular?... There comes a time when one must take the position that is neither safe, nor politic, nor popular, but he must do it because his conscience tells him it is right." [16]

Two thousand years ago, Paul wrote a letter to the Gentiles in Rome and said, in essence, that we have to be teammates. Specifically, he said,

"Because of the privilege and authority God has given me, I give each of you this warning: Don't think you are better than you really are. Be honest in your evaluation of yourselves, measuring yourselves by the faith God has given us. Just as our bodies have many parts and each part has a special function, so it is with Christ's body. We are many parts of one body, and we all belong to each other. In his grace, God has given us different gifts for doing certain things well. So if God has given you the ability to prophesy, speak out with as much faith as God has given you." (Romans 12:3-6)

Americans are a diverse lot of many ethnicities and religions but we are all on the same team. If we expect to stay "Number One" and care for our kids, we must find common ground. We must focus on what binds us together because we need every American on our team.

MIRACLE ON ICE

At the 1980 Winter Olympics, the Soviet Union's men's hockey team entered the Lake Placid games as the heavy favorite, having won the previous four ice hockey gold medals. Because of the Cold War, the Soviet and American teams had been rivals for decades. Moreover, President Carter was considering a U.S. boycott of the 1980 Moscow Summer Olympics in protest of the December 1979 Soviet invasion of

Afghanistan, and eventually decided in favor of the boycott. With that as the backdrop, the gold medal was between the U.S. and the U.S.S.R.

Not until there were ten minutes left in the game did Team USA take its first lead of the game. As the crowd began to count down the seconds left, Sportscaster Al Michaels picked up on the countdown in his broadcast, and delivered his famous call: "*Five seconds left in the game. Do you believe in miracles? Yes!*" What made the unexpected victory, forever referred to as the "Miracle on Ice," such an amazing upset was that the U.S. team was young and not that particularly talented, yet they defeated a team that was superior in every facet.

The United States is stronger when it "plays" together. We are not victorious because of certain superstars; we are successful because of a balancing act of talent, sacrifice and determination. To end the gridlock, stagnation, and dysfunction that sometimes paralyzes our country, we must as citizens ask, "Is it right?" and then our government leaders must, working together, act on everyone's behalf, instead of narrow constituencies, and enact laws that will benefit every member of Team America. If our leaders do not do so, if they pit one segment of society against another because it pleases a small percentage of their political base, or if they are free-range chickens with no governing philosophy other than serving themselves, principled people must speak up and insist and demand that we are one nation, that we are one people. We are in unchartered territory to some degree with Trump's cult of personality. Unless we accept that every single person has been created in God's image, and unless we have a 100% America, nothing will ever get done and every single American will suffer, including the rich and powerful. America has always been great, but we can be even greater if we work together.

12

IS IT TRUE?

"I am not bound to win but I am bound to be true. I am not bound to succeed, but I am bound to live by the light that I have. I must stand with anybody that stands right and stand with him while he is right and part with him when he goes wrong."
Abraham Lincoln

"let your good deeds shine out for all to see, so that everyone will praise your heavenly Father."
Jesus, Matthew 5:16

"Clean up your own mess."
All I Really Need to Know I Learned in Kindergarten

In January 1969, Joe Namath, the brash young quarterback of the New York Jets, made a bold and provocative prediction. He "guaranteed" that his team would defeat the heavily favored Baltimore Colts in the Super

Bowl that year. At that time, Namath and the Jets were from that "upstart" football league, the American Football League, or AFL, a league many regarded as lightweight and in no way the equal of the NFL, the National Football League. To the surprise of most in the sports world, and in Las Vegas, where the Colts were 18-19 point favorites, Namath delivered on his promise, leading the Jets to victory in a huge upset, making it one of the more memorable and colorful acts in sports history.

Whether Namath was truly prophetic, or merely brash and lucky, his prediction turned out to be true. Our politicians today, and especially Donald Trump, often say things that are not true. If we are to remain a world power for the indefinite future, we must insist on truth in every aspect of our society, including the White House.

THE TRUTH WILL SET YOU FREE

For many years, I was involved with Rotary International, a service organization founded over a century ago where people join local clubs so that they can serve their community. There are over 35,000 clubs world-wide that provide over 16 million volunteer hours each year.

Every year, my old district, which encompasses San Diego, holds a speech contest for local students, the topic being Rotary's Four-Way Test. The test is simple: "Of the things we think, say and do," 1) Is it the **truth**? 2) Is it **fair** to all concerned? 3) Will it build **goodwill** and **better friendships**? 4) Will it be **beneficial** to all concerned?

I think if our politicians asked these questions, our nation would be stronger and more prosperous. This chapter will focus on the first question: Is it the truth?

Although it has often been misinterpreted, Jesus once said that "*truth will set you free*" while Mark Twain once said, "*When in doubt, tell the truth. It will astound your enemies and confound your friends.*" America was built on a premise of honesty. "*I cannot tell a lie,*" George Washington supposedly said, when called out about who chopped down the family cherry tree. Abraham Lincoln, our greatest president, in my opinion, was nicknamed Honest Abe. Of course, politicians, and especially presidents lie, even our most admired ones.

Trump said that we would get tired of all the "winning." I, for one, am not sick of all the winning. I am, however, sick of all the excuses, finger-pointing, chaos, and lying.

AN EYE FOR AN EYE

Just after the election, I posted the story below on Facebook:

Hillary Clinton and Donald Trump both went for walks one day in October 2016 to get away from the brutal campaign trail. To their amazement, both ran into a genie, Clinton first and Trump a few hours later and were told they could have one wish. However, both were told that whatever they wished for, their opponent would get the same wish doubled. Initially taken aback by this bizarre caveat, both made the same wish: to be blind in one eye.

The above story is obviously not true, but since we live in hyper-partisan times where the opposite party is perceived as the enemy, or even an agent of the devil, there is some ring of truth in this tale. I frequently and vigorously disagree with Donald Trump and find many of his statements offensive, but I respect the office of the President and I realize he won the election. Therefore, I am praying for his success and I hope that others will as well.

If Trump follows the Constitution and acknowledges that he is but one part of an ingeniously designed system, I will respect him, even if I disagree with specific policies. But, if he does not,

I will not blindly follow, and I would encourage that regardless of your party, that you do not either, and hold him (and other politicians of both parties) accountable.

While Trump has been the Commander-in-Chief for only a short time, I am alarmed at the many untrue comments that have come from him and his officials. There is simply no such thing as alternate facts. People are, of course, entitled to their own opinions, but not to their own facts. Facts are facts and to suggest otherwise creates an Orwellian 1984 atmosphere where black is white and where words like "doublethink" and "newspeak" take on a life of their own. (It's not a coincidence that George Orwell's 1948 novel returned to the best-seller's list shortly after the election). In Orwell's book, the Ministry of Truth worked with three slogans: "War is peace. Freedom is slavery. Ignorance is strength," but in 2016 America, words and truth matter.

In Proverbs 6:16-19, seven things are described that are detestable to God. Two of those things involve being untruthful: a lying tongue and a false witness who pours out lies. If the Trump Administration is not truthful, all Americans, and especially Christians, must speak up and hold it accountable and not be blind followers. It's still early but his few months do not bode well for truthfulness. Fact checkers at The Washington Post catalogued 24 false or misleading statements made by the president during his first seven days and were amazed at the pattern: "mystifying false statements about seemingly trivial details, the rewriting of history to airbrush unwanted facts, the branding as liars those who point out his untruths, and a deft conversion of demonstrably false claims into a semantic mush of unverifiable beliefs."

"We've never seen anything this bizarre in our lifetimes, where up is down and down is up and everything is in question and

nothing is real," said Charles Lewis, the founder of the Center for Public Integrity and the author of 935 Lies: The Future of Truth and the Decline of America's Moral Integrity, a book about presidential deception. Steve Schmidt, who helped manage Senator John McCain's 2008 presidential campaign, said in an interview that Mr. Trump's cascade of falsehoods was "a direct assault on the very idea of representative democracy" in the United States.

He won the election and it is only fair that he be given a chance. I'm merely pointing out that extreme partisanship is counterproductive because it falsely finds fault, and even evil, in everything the opposition says and does while blindly overlooking fault within one's own party. If Trump honors the Constitution, I will applaud him and encourage others to do so as well.

In a democratic government, there must be truth in order to hold elected officials accountable to their sovereign (the people). It is my sincere hope that President Trump succeeds and I will continue to pray for him, but we elected a president, not a king. As he pointed out in his inaugural speech, he now works for all Americans, including those who did not vote for him. Regardless of party, let's pray for and support, but not blindly follow, our new president, and demand that our Administration presents the truth at all times and not alternate facts. Let's be truth-seeking and God-fearing patriots rather than blind partisans because an eye for an eye makes the whole country blind.

I received some criticism from that post, including from Christians who stated that Trump had been anointed by God and that we shouldn't criticize. I was stunned and have spent countless hours since trying to understand this widely held belief. What was I missing?

POST-TRUTH WORLD

In court proceedings, judges give instructions to the jury about what they are supposed to do during a trial and how to do it. In California, jury instruction 5003 addresses "Witnesses" and tells the jury how they are supposed to deal with them. It says in relevant part: *"if you decide a witness did not tell the truth about something important, you may choose not to believe anything that witness said."*[1]

Since Trump has said so many false things, how is anyone supposed to believe anything he says? Both the *New York Times* and the *Washington Post* have fact-checkers to examine many of the Administration's claims. The *Post* counted nearly 500 lies or misleading statements from the president alone in just his first 100 days.[2] The *Toronto Star* reported 18 misstatements or lies just from one Trump appearance in Iowa.[3] As mentioned in Chapter Two, in June 2017, the *New York Times* published a stunning article, cataloging Trump's lies by the day. The president, the piece said, is *"trying to create an atmosphere in which reality is irrelevant."*[4]

On August 2, 2017, the White House pushed back on accusations from reporters that President Trump lied about phone calls he said he received from the Mexican president and the leader of the Boy Scouts, both of whom quickly denied the president's claims.

Trump said at a Cabinet meeting that he had received a phone call from Mexican President Enrique Pena a Nieto praising his policies cracking down on illegal immigration into the U.S. *"And even the president of Mexico called me — they said their southern border, very few people are coming because they know they're not going to get through our border, which is the ultimate compliment."* The president also said in an interview with *The Wall Street Journal* that the head of the Boy Scouts had called him to thank him for a speech that generated much controversy for its inappropriate content. *"I got a call from the head of the Boy Scouts saying it was the greatest speech that was ever made to them, and they were very thankful."*

Both Mexico and the Boy Scouts denied such calls. At a press conference on August 2, a reporter asked the White House press secretary *"Why did the president say that he received a phone call from the leader of the Boy Scouts and the president of Mexico when he did not?"*[5]

It wasn't until both Mexico and the Boy Scouts denied the President's claims that the White House acknowledged that, well, he didn't actually talk to either of them. Sarah Huckabee Sanders said that Trump "misspoke" – that he did not receive phone calls but rather had personal conversations. Regarding Mexico, Trump was referring to a personal conversation he had with the Mexican president at the previous month's G-20 summit. Regarding the Boy Scouts, Trump did not actually hear from the president directly, but rather that he had heard from "multiple members of Boy Scout leadership" who offered him "quite powerful compliments."

"So he lied," the reporter shot back. *"That's a pretty bold accusation,"* Sanders said with indignation and then slithered through an explanation that could at best be called baloney.

It's not the specific lie that matters; what matters is that these misstatements reveal that Trump views the truth subjectively. He consistently bends reality to fit how he *wants* it to be. The Boy Scouts *did* in fact cheer him, right? The only conclusion, therefore, is that its leader thought he was the best. It doesn't matter whether it actually happened or not. What matters is that it *felt* like it happened. Therefore, it must be true.

The problem is that whatever it is that you might see, or think you see, isn't the same thing as "real" truth. Like the boy who called wolf, multiple false statements create a scenario that no one will believe you in the future even if you are telling the truth. So, if Trump is willing to lie about something so trivial as these phone calls, or crowd size, or whatever, why should we believe anything he says?

Trump frequently will say, as he did in his August 2017 rally in Arizona, something like: "*I really believe…,*" as he did about the media. "*They hate our country, I really believe.*" Since there is no tie-in to actual truth, people who like him can accept it as true even without any basis or proof. I really believe that millions of Americans really believe whatever Donald Trump really believes even though there is no evidence to support what is really believed. To counter this, Bernie Sanders, Elizabeth Warren, and others will say that they really believe the exact opposite and their supporters will really believe that version as well. The next thing you know, there's no such thing as truth and whether somebody is to be believed, or whether somebody obstructed justice, or whether somebody hates our country, or whether there was massive electoral fraud, depends solely on whether they are a Democrat or Republican.

GOD HATES A LYING TONGUE

Since lying is clearly something that God hates, why are Christians not bothered by Trump's constant lying? Why are they not outraged? In a thought-provoking article in *Christian Ethics Today* in February 2017 called *"What Lies Within: Post-Truth Evangelical Christianity,"* Bruce Gourley examined this very issue of why Christians don't seem bothered by the constant stream of lies spewing from the White House. Below are some excerpts:

> *"From his long-voiced racist lie about Barack Obama being born in Kenya to his designation by fact-checking organizations as far and away the greatest liar of any presidential candidate they had ever examined, Donald Trump routinely and brashly flaunted his disdain for the truth. Even so, the Republican candidate courted evangelicals with promises of political favoritism. Robert Jeffress, abandoning earlier assertions that a presidential candidate's faith mattered, spoke for a growing majority of evangelicals in the summer of 2016 who were desperate for a return to*

political power. Jeffress declared: 'You know, I was debating an evangelical professor on NPR, and this professor said, "Pastor, don't you want a candidate who embodies the teaching of Jesus and would govern this country according to the principles found in the Sermon on the Mount?" I said, "Heck no." I would run from that candidate as far as possible, because the Sermon on the Mount was not given as a governing principle for this nation.'" [6]

So, just to be clear, Christians, according to Jeffress, don't want their president to exhibit any of the principles articulated by their Lord and Savior. Does that mean that the standard, then, for a politician is to act the opposite of Jesus? I would not support such a standard.

"At the same time, evangelicals also applauded many of the candidate's most obvious lies... In addition, evangelicals voiced no discernible concern about Trump's own history of employing illegal immigrants, outsourcing American jobs to foreign countries, or his track record of some 4,000 or so lawsuits resulting from his shoddy, illegal, or otherwise unethical business practices," Gourley continued.

"When journalists pointed out the falseness of Trump's statements, evangelicals, preconditioned to false narratives, found comfort in their world of fake news that embraced self-serving lies as desired truth. In other words, 2016 was the year of crowd-sourced lies, false narratives that especially resonated with evangelical Christians who no longer valued reality or truth that ran counter to their personal beliefs. Safely ensconced within their alternative world, they condemned or ignored truths reported by the mainstream media." [7]

In its January/February 2017 issue, *Politico* magazine acknowledged that all politicians lie but added a caveat. *"But Donald Trump is in a different category. The sheer frequency, spontaneity, and seeming irrelevance of his lies have no precedent. Nixon, Reagan, and Clinton were protecting their reputations; Trump seems to lie for the pure joy of it.*"[8]

In his own autobiography, Trump used the phrase "truthful hyperbole," a term coined by his ghostwriter referring to the flagrant truth-stretching that Trump employed, over and over, to help close sales. Trump apparently loved the wording and went on to adopt it as his own. Trump takes it even further. If he has a particular untruth he wants to focus on, he simply repeats it over and over. Repeated statements are much more likely to be accepted as real the more they are heard, no matter their actual validity. If you repeatedly, say, for example, that there was voter fraud, that you were against the war in Iraq, or that your tax bill is the biggest in history, the actual truth matters less. Even worse, as some fear, is that if we stop reacting to Trump's lies then his lying becomes normalized. We might even become more likely to lie ourselves. Trump is creating a highly politicized landscape where everyone is either for him or against him and where the thinking never extends beyond if you win, I lose, and vice versa.

That is a sad and scary scenario and we must never let it happen.

"GET OVER IT"

As recounted in *Abraham Lincoln's Classroom*, Lincoln was campaigning for Congress in 1846 against an opponent named Peter Cartwright. Cartwright was known for evading questions and Lincoln would often remark that Cartwright reminded him of a hunter he once knew who recognized the fact that in summer the deer were red and in winter gray. Therefore, there was a season when a deer might resemble a calf. "*The hunter had brought down one at long range when it was hard to see the difference,*" Lincoln said, "*and boasting of his own marksmanship had said: 'I shot at it so as to hit it if it was a deer and miss it if it was a calf.'*"[9]

Sounds like something Trump would have said. Although he didn't speak out immediately after Charlottesville because he was "waiting to get all the facts," he immediately proclaimed that the violence in Barcelona in August 2017 was due to terrorism. When authorities confirmed that was the case, Trump congratulated himself on being right. When Egypt Air MS804 disappeared over the Mediterranean on May 19, 2016, Trump immediately proclaimed terrorism as well. However, after an exhaustive investigation, authorities declared it in May 2017 to have been an accident. Trump, however, has never admitted he was wrong.

Trump even channels Austrian physicist Erwin Schrodinger, who, in an experiment on quantum mechanics, postulated that a cat inside a sealed box could be both alive and dead. In February 2017, Trump, at a rally in Florida, said the following: "*You look at what's happening. We've got to keep our country safe. You look at what's happening in Germany, you look at what's happening last night in Sweden.*" Since nothing had happened "last night," Trump was widely ridiculed for this would-be terrorist act. When an actual terrorist attack occurred two months later, the new interpretation of Trump's February comments was that he had predicted it. Therefore, you cannot only shoot a deer and a calf at the same time, have a cat that is both alive and dead at the same time, but you can also have peace and terrorism at the same time.

Trump's lies are so frequent that many have given up and are now arguing that we should just *get over it*. The argument is that while everyone knows he lies, his supporters and admirers simply don't care and that they take him seriously but not literally. I refuse to "get over it" and I look to the Bible, the Declaration of Independence and the Boy Scout law. Proverbs 12:22 says, "*The Lord detests lying lips but he delights in people who are trustworthy.*"

The Declaration states that we all have the right to life, liberty, and the pursuit of happiness and that to secure these rights, governments are instituted, deriving their power from the consent of the governed. If my government does not tell the truth, then it does not have my consent. If the government lacks the consent of the people, its powers are not just. Donald Trump and the other leaders of the U.S. government are entitled to their opinions, which I realize may be different than mine. They are not entitled to their own facts. The Boy Scout law lists twelve characteristics of a scout: *"A scout is trustworthy, loyal, helpful, friendly, courteous, kind, obedient, cheerful, thrifty, brave, clean and reverent."* While being thrifty and clean are important, notice the first value listed: trustworthy.

If our leaders lie and equivocate, we must demand that they change course and tell us the plain unvarnished, non-partisan truth whether they "really" believe it or not. To those who love this country, and especially to those who claim to follow Jesus Christ, it is not possible to ignore the constant lying coming out of the White House. Honest mistakes, and even negligence, can be excused. Regardless of your tribe, deliberate deception cannot ever be accepted or tolerated.

13

WOULD JESUS APPROVE?

"When I do good, I feel good. When I do bad, I feel bad. That's my religion."
Abraham Lincoln

"But anyone who hears my teaching and doesn't obey it is foolish, like a person who builds a house on the sand."
Jesus, Matthew 7:26

"Wash your hands before you eat."
All I Really Need to Know I Learned in Kindergarten

In 1982, Miles McPherson, a defensive back from the University of New Haven, was drafted by the Los Angeles Rams, fulfilling a life-long dream of playing in the NFL. McPherson would go onto to play four years in the NFL with the Rams and the San Diego Chargers.

McPherson had become a fixture in the party scene and often spent a good part of his salary on cocaine that he put up his nose. In April of 1984, he gave that up in a single day and dedicated his life to Jesus Christ. McPherson finally worked his way into the starting line-up for the Chargers and it looked like he had a bright future. On a Monday night game against the Los Angeles Raiders, in front of a nationwide audience, McPherson's dreams came to a crashing halt as he suffered a knee injury that knocked him out for the season. Although he came back to play again, for all intents and purposes, his career ended that night. McPherson had just recently become a saved Christian and spoke unabashedly about his faith to anyone who would listen. As he was being carried off the field that Monday night, many of the players had looks on their faces that seemed to say, *"Where is your God now?"*

After showers, the Chargers got on the team buses and headed off for the two-hour drive to San Diego. McPherson sat in the aisle seat next to the team doctor with his leg blocking the aisle. McPherson didn't know what his future held but he knew that he had this doctor captive for the next two hours. So, instead of whining about his bad luck, McPherson witnessed to the doctor about the Lord Jesus Christ. For the last thirty-plus years, he has done the same to anyone who would listen.

McPherson's career ended in 1985 and he had no idea what he was going to do. He enrolled in Azusa Pacific University's School of Theology and received a Master's of Divinity in 1991. Today, he is the Senior Pastor of the Rock Church in San Diego, one of the largest churches in the United States, with over 15,000 congregants. For many years, I attended the Rock Church and have been honored to call Pastor Miles my pastor because he constantly challenged me to reject false prophets, also known as fake news, in favor of the one who is true.

REDEMPTION

As I've stated, I am a devout Christian and believe that Jesus was the son of God, but I realize that may Americans do not. While Christians have been commanded to share what they know with others about the "Good News," I will not do so in this book. That is another argument for another day. I firmly believe in the separation of church and state and this book is about politics. However, certain Christian principles and certain statements by Jesus have shaped my life and I believe that they can be utilized to foster better government. While Jesus said and did many things, his life could be reduced to two elements: 1) showing us how to get to heaven through being redeemed and 2) showing us how to live better lives here on earth by loving, serving, and helping others and asking, in essence, *"Where does it hurt?"* While this country is made up of many religions, one of our unshakeable precepts is that this country is predicated on belief in a supreme being.

Can the United States be redeemed and released from its chains? Absolutely. Despite a trend towards secularization, the Supreme Court has continuously acknowledged the role of God through its decisions and this must never change. To this day, sessions of the Supreme Court open with the prayer: *"God save the United States and this Honorable Court."* Writing that the *"history of man is inseparable from the history of religion,"* the Court has permitted state legislatures to open their daily sessions with a prayer by a chaplain paid by the state. Since 1935, there has been a depiction of Moses holding two stone tablets that reveal portions of the Ten Commandments, along with other lawgivers, in the Supreme Court courtroom.

Overlooking the rotunda of the Library of Congress' Jefferson Building is a large statute of Moses holding the Ten Commandments alongside a statute of the Apostle Paul. In front of the Ronald Reagan Building is another sculpture that includes a depiction of the Ten Commandments. Additionally, a 24-foot tall sculpture depicting, among other things, the Ten Commandments and a cross, stands outside the federal courthouse that houses both the Court of Appeals and the District Court for the

District of Columbia. Moses is also prominently featured in the Chamber of the House of Representatives.

The Framers clearly believed that morality and virtue were important and that organized religion played an important role in cultivating this virtue. John Adams stated in 1789, *"Our Constitution was made only for a moral and religious people. It is wholly inadequate to the government of any other."*[1] Thomas Jefferson concluded his second inaugural address by inviting his audience to pray.

The separation of church and state began in 1776 when the thirteen colonies, reborn as states, replaced their colonial charters granted by the king with written constitutions deriving their authority from the consent of the governed. In the generations after the Revolution, most of America's new citizens were Christian, although from different sects. Due to increasing friction between the various groups, a "non-sectarian Christianity" was created. However, intense fighting erupted for many decades over parochial schools and the role of the Bible in public schools. In the late 19th and early 20th centuries, Darwinism inspired many to advocate atheism and subsequently, large numbers of Jewish immigrants changed the dynamics once again.

When World War II ended, the baby boom period saw enormous growth in churches across the country. As the Cold War began, it became commonplace to speak of "Godless communism" as the number one enemy. In 1954, Congress added the words "Under God" to the Pledge and in 1956, Congress declared "In God We Trust" as the national motto.[2]

In case after case, however, the Supreme Court suggested that religion ought to be disentangled from the public sphere. In 1962, the High Court held that prayer in public school classrooms violated the Constitution. A year later, the Court found that reading of the Bible in school also violated the Constitution. These decisions infuriated people of faith and the pendulum swung back as the Moral Majority and the Christian Coalition came forward.

The result of these two movements is the sharp cultural divide that we know today. Neither side is able to reconcile religious diversity and national unity. Evangelicals dispute that government funding of religion creates disunity, rather than unity, while secularists insist that we totally separate religion from government, although this necessarily excludes many citizens.

Author Jon Meachem wrote in *American Gospel*, "*Our finest hour – the Revolutionary War, abolition, the expansion of the rights of women, fights against terror and tyranny, the battle against Jim Crow – can partly be traced to religious ideas about liberty, justice, and charity.*"[3] Often, religion creates division and conflict and, as Meachem points out, "*Yet theology and scripture have also been used to justify our worst hours – from enslaving black people to persecuting Native Americans to treating women as second-class citizens.*"[4]

The Puritans came to this country to carry out what they believed was God's will to live righteously. The Puritans, believing that tolerance was a sin, excluded those who thought differently than they did. The problem for the Puritans was that other people "kept showing up" and, instead of trying to adapt, they tried to outlaw it. 400 years later, many of us are doing the same thing. As Meachem says, "*If the Lord himself chose not to force obedience from those he created, then who are men to try?*"[5]

The argument that politics must remain secular in order to not be exclusive is flawed because it necessarily excludes citizens of faith. On the other hand, Evangelicals seek unity by actively promoting certain religious values, even though not everyone agrees on these values. Perhaps there is a solution, as set forth by Noah Feldman in *Divided By God*. We must abandon the argument that religion has no place in the public arena. It does, and we must insist that government not support any particular religious institutions. Basically, the state may not coerce anyone in matters of religion nor expend resources to support religious institutions and practices. As Feldman says, *"No coercion and no money."*[6]

Secularists have argued that public displays of religion reduce everyone's ability to participate in a common national public life. As Feldman points out, there is nothing exclusive about one group exercising its religious beliefs. As long as Michael Newdow, who sued to remove "Under God" from the Pledge of Allegiance, is not coerced into reciting the Pledge, it makes no sense to bar others from reciting words that he alone finds exclusionary. Furthermore, when secularists overshoot, Feldman explains, it creates resentment on the part of the Evangelicals and a reactionary attempt to impose new symbols, like the Ten Commandments in courthouses, where none existed before. In turn, strident actions and comments by Evangelicals create the same whiplash effect by secularists, and the back-and-forth pendulum never ceases.

Americans will never all agree on who God is, but we should be able to agree on who *we* are. People live their lives trying, among other things, to find truth and what is good. Once we find what we believe to be the truth, it's only human nature that we should express our discovery publicly. We are within our rights to stand our ground and insist that everyone else is wrong. They are free to shout to the mountaintops that our beliefs are absolute drivel.

AM I MY BROTHER'S KEEPER?

When Christians think politics, it generally means abortion, gay marriage, pornography, and "religious freedom." However, there are other political issues that both the Bible and Jesus address. In the first chapter of the Bible, Cain asked, *"Am I my brother's keeper?"* The answer is yes, you are accountable for whatever you do to those that are made in the image of God.

While we can all do our part individually, government is the vehicle through which the largest number of people can be reached. God is in favor of government. The Bible highlights God-fearing men and women who served in public office. Deborah served as judge over Israel, Joseph served as prime minister for the Egyptian Pharaoh, Daniel served in the court of Nebuchadnezzar's Babylon, and Nehemiah was a trusted official for the Persian king Artaxerxes. Jesus paid taxes and encouraged his disciples to do the same. Government wasn't always friendly to Christians in the Roman era but Paul encouraged submission to the governing authorities who are "ministers of God" and to whom taxes, respect, and honor were owed. Peter also told believers that part of their service to the common good was to fear God and honor the Roman emperor. These examples confirm that government has always been part of God's plan.

When Jesus began his very public and political life, he was constantly helping the poor and the disabled, including lepers. He crossed racial and ethnic lines in his dealings with Samaritans and did not care what the established laws were about work on the Sabbath. He just wanted to help and heal others. In his teachings, he said *"Blessed are the poor, the meek, the mourning, the peacemakers, and the persecuted."* The early church followed his example. They built the first hospitals and orphanages and developed systems of adoption. They built churches to care for needs and to develop better citizens for the world. Later, a number of Christians would be influential in forming this nation around the Biblical themes of freedom and liberty.

When it comes to politics, the Bible gives us no reason to believe Jesus would side completely with one political viewpoint over another. Interestingly, there was political diversity among Jesus's disciples. Included in the twelve were Simon, a left-wing zealot, and Matthew, a right-wing tax collector. Zealots worked *against* the government while tax collectors worked *for* the government. Despite their opposing political viewpoints, Matthew and Simon were friends. Moreover, when it came to kings and kingdoms, Jesus sided only with himself. In the book that bears his name, Joshua headed into battle and encountered the angel of the Lord. Joshua asked him if he was for them or for their adversaries. The angel of the Lord didn't specifically answer the question and simply replied that he was the Commander of the Army of the Lord.

Is the opposing party an enemy to be crushed? Wouldn't it be better to persuade people who disagree with you that your ways are better through logic, mastery of the subject matter and empathy for their side of the story? Wouldn't it be better if your brother in the other party, who had been misguided and dead, like the Prodigal Son, had come back to life? If he had been lost, would you not want him to change his position and "be found?"

Naïve, you might say. Unrealistic, the majority will proclaim. Join the real world, others will argue. As I've said several times, I know that everyone will not suddenly hold hands and sing songs around the camp fire. One-sided hard line positions never work in the long run. Democrats are quick to point this out now but quickly forget this lesson when they get back in power. So, the best party leaders can hope for is to achieve a short-term success at the expense of the other party, which not only breeds hatred and resentment, but is overturned when an election changes the political composition. I know that partisanship will never completely disappear or be completely eliminated, but wouldn't it be better if we could avoid much of its counter-productive waste and inefficiency and work out long-term solutions?

WHERE DOES IT HURT?

In beginning his three-year ministry, Jesus came to Nazareth, the town where he grew up, to the synagogue where he worshipped and read from the Prophet Isaiah:

"The Spirit of the Lord is upon me, for he has anointed me to bring good news to the poor. He has sent me to proclaim that captives will be released, that the blind will see, that the oppressed will be set free, and that the time of the Lord's favor has come." (Luke 4:18-19)

These words are often described as his inaugural address where he outlined his politics and established his priorities: good news to the poor, release to the captive, sight to the blind, letting the oppressed go free, declaring God's favor. At the heart of Jesus' politics is an unspoken question: where does it hurt? As Jesus would later say, *"Those who are well have no need of a physician, but those who are sick."* (Luke 5:31)

What if we began our political thinking and conversations not by asking *"Who's sleeping with whom?"* or *"what's in it for me?"* but by asking, *"Where does it hurt?"* What if we let that question establish our priorities and guide our decisions? Compassion would be the primary concern. It would take courage to stand with others in their pain and we would have to be vulnerable enough to risk letting others stand with us in our pain, but wouldn't it be better than ripping each other apart? I realize that this is not easy but all things are possible through God.

How would Jesus react to the homeless, to poverty, to human trafficking, to drug addiction, to racism? Would he would disregard them and focus on bathrooms and wedding cakes? While he would certainly be a pro-life advocate, would he not also be an advocate for single mothers unable to care for their kids? Would he not be a proponent for adoptions? Would he not encourage us to love others rather than condemn? Would Jesus favor tax cuts for the rich? Would he be in favor of pollution? Would he simply accept that 20% of people should not have health insurance? Would he support threats of starting nuclear war or actually starting one? Would he be supportive of leaving the next generation with $21 trillion of debt?

Jesus provided us the way to get to heaven but for three years he also taught us how to live on earth by helping, serving, and loving each other. Many claim that they want a Christian government, but a government based on the teachings of Jesus Christ would be premised on this foundational question: *"Where does it hurt?"* Everything else flows from this perspective-altering question. Jesus also said if you want to gain your life, you have to lose it, that to be first, you have to be last, that to achieve victory, you have to surrender, and to truly live, you have to die. These concepts are radical and counter to what the world teaches, but rather than being based on the Trumpian belief that if you lose, I win, it's based on if you win, I win, too. To keep America great, let's not just ask, *"What's in it for me?"* but *"Where does it hurt?"*

14

IS IT GOOD FOR OUR KIDS?

"All that I am or hope to be, I owe to my angel mother."
Abraham Lincoln

"Let the children come to me. Don't stop them. For the Kingdom of God belongs to those who are like these children."
Jesus, Mark 10:14

"Put things back where you found them."
All I Really Need to Know I Learned in Kindergarten

According to Dave Zirin, the sports editor for *The Nation* magazine, Nov. 17, 1968 is when the modern age of football began.[1] The New York Jets were playing the Oakland Raiders, two of the best teams in the American Football League, just before it merged with the National Football League. Although I was quite young, and did not really understand football, I remember watching that game that day with my dad from our home in Florida.

It was a close game as the lead changed six times before it was all tied up, 29 to 29. Then, Jim Turner kicked a 26-yard field goal and the Jets took the lead as the clock was winding down. With 50 seconds remaining, Raiders quarterback Daryle Lamonica hit Charlie Smith on a 20-yard pass, and after a penalty, the Raiders crossed midfield. All of a sudden, my dad and I, along with millions of other people, saw a little blond girl with braids in the Swiss Alps walking down a hill instead of the Raiders and the Jets. I didn't understand what was happening as my dad went ballistic. As it turned out, the Raiders made a thrilling comeback with two touchdowns in the last 50 seconds. Most of the country, though, including my dad and I, missed it because the network had scheduled the made-for-television children's movie *Heidi* at precisely 7 p.m.

We would later find out that the phone banks at NBC were flooded with thousands of furious fans, completely jamming the switchboards. The uproar from what became known as the "Heidi Game" changed the way the networks covered NFL games and never again would the NFL cut away to scheduled programming if a game ran late.

The thing I remember was that I didn't really like football at the time and I wanted to watch *Heidi* but my dad, a huge football fan, wouldn't let me and was ready to spontaneously combust. Oftentimes, our politicians are like my dad, oblivious to what kids want and need. I think that the policies of the U.S. government should, to the extent possible, try to consider the millions of people under 18 that live in this country.

NEIL ARMSTRONG AND THE PURPOSE OF LIFE

When I was 12, my father took my brother and I to see Apollo 11 blast off for the moon from Cape Kennedy, 60 miles from our home in Daytona Beach, Florida. I was awestruck as the giant rocket spewed out huge balls of fire, shook the ground and started its ascension towards the heavens. Three days later I watched in amazement as Neil Armstrong took a giant leap for mankind a quarter of a million miles away from earth.

Five years later, I headed off to college. I was then, and remain today, a proud member of the Florida Gator nation. I learned a few things during my four years at UF and they gave me a diploma but I never contemplated the meaning of life or pondered what my purpose might be. My life was very simple. I studied, played intramural basketball, went to football games, drank beer, constantly thought about going out with girls (but rarely did) and hung out with my friends. I didn't have a car (which partially explains my infrequent dates) and I rode my bike everywhere. I knew nothing of the "real" world and although I went to church every Sunday, I didn't really know why other than Catholics were supposed to.

As the years zipped by, I served in the army, taught college, spent 30 years as an attorney, and often asked myself that imponderable question: what's the point of it all? Raising my two kids was the highlight of my life, but they are now adults and on their own. For years, my life was a never-ending stream of basketball, football, soccer, baseball, gymnastics, Girl Scouts, band, YMCA campouts, parent-teacher conferences, etc. I coached my son's basketball teams, was the president of the PTA at my kids' elementary school, and of the many hats I wore, "dad" was the most important one. When my son left for college in 2012, I was shocked at the huge void that I experienced. For years, my family was my life, but my family was now gone and for the first time in decades, I felt lost.

Below are excerpts from a letter I wrote to my daughter, Rachel, when she turned 18.

Life is like a diamond with four points. You comprise two points, other people make up one, and the fourth point is God. The reason that you make up two points is both simple and complex. You not only interact with other people and God, you interact with yourself in multiple ways. You do so by seeking certain positive things, such as wisdom, truth, courage and justice, and by avoiding certain negative things, such as fear, greed, and pride. You also interact with your past self as well as your future self. Do not make the mistake of many young people and think that the world started in the 1990s. Despite the wonders of technology, King Solomon was right, in a sense, when he said three thousand years ago that there is nothing new under the sun. People are basically the same as they've always been. But also do not get so bogged down in your day to day life that you do not adequately plan for the future. Always move forward but remember that there's much wisdom to be gained from looking to the past, whether by studying history, examining your mistakes, or from seeking guidance from those older than you.

With the four points in mind, a successful life can be summed up as follows:

1) Have Faith in God,

2) Treat Others Well,

3) Do Your Best and Never Quit

When my son graduated from high school, this was the beginning of the letter I wrote:

Tomorrow you will take a big step towards becoming an adult by graduating from high school. Mommy, Rachel, and I are all very proud of you and believe that your future is very bright. Although I made mistakes, I tried my very best to be a good father and will continue to do so until the day I die. As I told Rachel when she graduated, life is complicated and there are millions of things that can overwhelm and absorb you. Life, therefore, is simply choosing and prioritizing. As I told Rachel, living a successful life has three components: 1) Have faith in God, 2) treat others well, and 3) do your best and never quit. I would suggest putting God first in your life, other people second, and yourself third. If you put yourself first, you'll never be satisfied and you'll never find your purpose because we were not put here to merely acquire wealth and be comfortable. If you were to gain the whole world, what good would it be if you forfeited your own soul? A person's life does not consist in the abundance of his possessions. You will have many important days in your life but the two most important are: 1) The day you were born, and 2) the day you figure out why.

I have made more than my share of mistakes and I am determined to help my kids, and kids like them throughout this country, figure out why they were born. I am determined that our government institute policies that will not harm them, will not debilitate them and will not crush their spirit. I am determined to help them achieve their hopes and dreams. I hope you are too.

MODERN SLAVERY

The bright summer sun blinded me as I tried to shield my eyes. I glanced around the pavilion that was erected for the college graduation of students at California State at San Marcos, one of which was my son, Riley. Riley and his classmates had worked hard for the last four years and today they would become college graduates. CSUSM, as it is called, is located north of San Diego and is home to 12,000 students. What made this day particularly exciting was that Riley had been selected to give a speech. His class had been asked to submit an essay and his essay, out of several thousand, was selected as the winner. I had asked him several times what it was about but he wouldn't give me a hint. "You'll see," was all he said.

Finally, the ceremony began. After several speeches by the University President and other dignitaries, Riley suddenly appeared on the stage and approached the podium to applause. I then noticed for the first time an old-fashioned wooden blockade on the stage. Suddenly, three other young adults, two girls and one boy, approached the blockade. One of the girls was dressed nicely and her hair was immaculate, but the boy and the other girl were dressed shabbily and looked like they hadn't showered in weeks. The three students suddenly put their heads and arms through the blockade and were now immobilized. I was puzzled and I noticed that many in the crowd had the same reaction to this unexpected development. As the crowd became eerily silent, Riley began to speak.

"Good morning, Madame President, members of the board of trustees, professors, my fellow students, ladies and gentlemen. My name is Riley Hester. I was born and raised in San Diego and have worked very hard the last four years to get to this place. Although I received excellent training from my professors, all that I am today and all that I have achieved is due to my mother and father," Riley said as I beamed with pride. *"Their love, patience and respect gave me a soft, compassionate, and gentle side. The ability to empathize, to understand the frailties and weaknesses of people, has helped me immensely these last four years but, more importantly, their demands and challenges, their insistence on excellence, countered my compassionate side with a tough and demanding one. All people, especially leaders, need both of these qualities if they are to succeed. The 'dark' side, if you will, allows for decisiveness and ambition, for discipline and toughness. When combined with the 'good' side, it results in a potent force.*

"My particular topic today is the Fourth of July, a holiday that we will be celebrating in a few weeks for the 242nd time since July 4, 1776. Our future president, Thomas Jefferson, only 32 years-old at the time, wrote these eloquent words:

'We hold these truths to be self-evident, that all men are created equal, that they are endowed by their Creator with certain inalienable rights, that among these are Life, Liberty and the pursuit of Happiness. That to secure these rights, Governments are instituted among men, deriving their just powers from the consent of the governed. That whenever any form of government becomes destructive of these ends, it is the right of the people to alter or abolish it and to institute new government...'"

Riley paused for a moment and smiled. I had no idea what was about to come.

"As you know, the Colonists had numerous complaints with King George and the British crown and Jefferson listed a couple of dozen grievances to justify to the world that the United States ought to be absolved of allegiance to the British Crown. And nearly two and a half centuries later, the United States is still standing and is the richest, freest and most powerful country in the world." The crowd vigorously applauded and Riley smiled again, but the next few words out of his mouth froze my feet to the ground.

"However, my friends and I are here to tell you that for millions of Americans, it's all a big lie." I felt like I had been kicked in the stomach. *"From the very beginning of our republic, there have been divisions. During the Constitutional Convention, the battle was between big states and small states, and later, between slave states and free states. At the beginning of the 20th century, the combatants were big business and the common man. Later, it was between black and white and then between people of faith and the secular world. But I'm here to tell you,"* he said slowly with an edge in his voice, *"today's battle is between young and old and rich and poor. In other words, between all of you and the four of us."*

Although I knew few people in the crowd, I felt they were all staring at me.

"Our government's policies have become destructive towards young and poor people and the Life, Liberty and pursuit of Happiness that Jefferson eloquently wrote of does not apply to us," Riley said, pausing. *"Please take a close look at my friends. One of them is also a graduating senior from this fine institution and grew up in an affluent home. The other two, however, never finished high school and have been sleeping on the streets of San Diego for the last several years."* A collective gasp from the crowd made me shiver.

"And so, let us submit facts to a candid world. The following is our list of grievances with the United States government, and since policies are made with the consent of the governed, these grievances apply to each of you as well.

1. *You have saddled our generation with a debt of over twenty trillion dollars, while demanding more tax cuts and more benefits.*

2. *Even though the Medicare system has been in a deficit for years, you still withdraw billions of dollars of benefits each year while many beneficiaries are millionaires.*

3. *Even though the Social Security system is now in the red, you have refused to make any reforms to the system, guaranteeing that none of us will ever receive any benefits.*

4. *Whatever the merits of the wars in Iraq and Afghanistan, those wars were paid for with borrowed money. The four of us, and not any of you, will have to pay it back.*

5. *The massive debt that you have saddled us with comes with massive interest. My generation will have to pay nearly two billion dollars a day in interest payments to our various creditors, including China.*

6. *The only way to pay for this debt is to dramatically decrease governmental services and to radically increase taxes. My generation will bear the brunt of this in the years to come.*

7. *In 2016, 60 million people lived in poverty in the U.S., an increase of 16% from last year. This shocking number is the largest number seen in the 58 years for which poverty estimates have been published. Never have so many Americans lived so poorly.*

8. *In 2016, 25% of all children lived in Poverty USA. That's 1 in every 4 children.*

9. *What's worse, 10% of the population — or nearly 35 million people — live in deep poverty, with incomes at only 50% of their poverty thresholds."*

I thought that I was going to pass out. Although I didn't think it possible, it got worse.

"Even though I love my dad, I'm sorry to say that he's a hypocrite. He's a Christian and is always telling me about Jesus and getting to heaven. But let's just talk about earth. I'm sure there are a bunch of Christians here today. Why aren't you speaking up about the massive debt that will debilitate us for decades to come? Why aren't you emulating your savior, Jesus, by heeding his words and helping the poor? The book of Proverbs says that the borrower becomes a slave to the lender. If you want to enslave yourselves, go ahead, but what gives you the right to enslave us? Through your selfishness, you've made us slaves." Turning towards his friends in the blockade, he continued.

"And since constant school-shootings, like the one in Parkland, Florida, and all over this country don't seem to bother you, it seems apparent that your guns are more important to you than our safety. But let me be clear: students don't want to be shot at school and millions of young Americans will vote officials out of office if they don't pass tougher laws."

I thought I was going to have an aneurism but he continued. *"In closing, I would like to recite part of a speech given on the Fourth of July in 1852 by Frederick Douglas, the nation's leading black abolitionist. And while*

Douglas was speaking of slaves based on race, his speech applies just as much today. Today's young and poor people are modern slaves and the slaveholders are all the self-absorbed baby boomers who blindly celebrate Independence Day while forgetting your obligations to posterity and all you Christians who ignore the three years that Jesus spent on earth."

"'Fellow citizens, pardon me, allow me to ask, why am I called upon to speak here today? What have I, or those I represent, to do with your national independence? Are the great principles of political freedom and of natural justice, embodied in that Declaration of Independence, extended to us?

But such is not the state of the case. I say it with a sad sense of disparity between us. I am not included within the pale of this glorious anniversary! Your high independence only reveals the immeasurable distance between us. The blessings in which you, this day, rejoice are not enjoyed in common. The rich inheritance of justice, liberty, prosperity and independence bequeathed by your fathers is shared by you, not by me. The sunlight that brought light and healing to you has brought stripes and death to me. This Fourth of July is yours, not mine. You may rejoice, I must mourn.

What, to the American slave, is your Fourth of July? I answer: a day that reveals to him, more than all other days in the year, the gross injustice and cruelty to which he is the constant victim. To him, your celebration is a sham; your boasted liberty, an unholy license; your national greatness, swelling vanity; your denunciation of tyrants, brass-fronted impudence, your shouts of liberty and equality, hollow mockery; your prayers and hymns, sermons and thanksgivings, with all your religious parade and solemnity, are, to Him, mere bombast, fraud, deception, impiety and hypocrisy-a thin veil to cover up crimes which would disgrace a nation of savages. There is not a nation of savages, there is not a nation on the earth guilty of practices more shocking and bloody than are the people of the United States at this very hour.'"[1]

Suddenly, I jumped up, my heart pounding, and I realized that I was in my bed. It had been a dream. Or, to be more accurate, the mother of all nightmares. Thank God. Although my dream was exaggerated hyperbole, there is considerable substance to the thoughts that meandered through my subconscious. As a result of our inability to work together, because of our constant fighting over things both great and small, and because of the baby boomers' insistence on more benefits and more tax cuts, along with our insatiable demand for guns, we are creating a world with two irreconcilable sides. Neither side will win and our children will lose, but it's not too late to straighten the ship.

I was once a candidate for Judge and participated in a forum with the media and the other candidates one night. The candidates were all asked a question. All were predictable except for mine, which came out of left field. *"Who is your hero?"* I was asked. For a moment, I froze but then I smiled as I realized it was an easy question. *"My mother,"* I answered. She sacrificed everything for my brother and I and put our needs ahead of her own. She was the most thoughtful and kind person I ever knew and she taught me about honesty and decency. I haven't always been successful but I have tried to be as good a parent to my kids as she was to me and whenever I think about myself, I try to think about my kids as well and how my decisions will affect them.

Are we making America a great place for all? Are we humbling ourselves like children like Jesus said to do? Are we giving children encouragement? Are we heroes to our kids? Let's not forget the next generation or saddle them with debilitating debt and let's strive to leave them a world better than the one we inherited. Let's make it a goal that we should individually, and as a nation, set examples for young people so that they can have success. Let's consider how our decisions will affect them and let's work as a team so that their future will be bright.

15

WOULD LINCOLN CONCUR?

"Do I not destroy my enemies when I make them my friends?"
Abraham Lincoln

"But I say, love your enemies! Pray for those who persecute you! In that way,
you will be acting as true children of your father in heaven."
Jesus, Matthew 5:44

"Put things back where you found them."
All I Really Need to Know I Learned in Kindergarten

The Walter Payton NFL Man of the Year award is presented annually honoring a player's volunteer and charity work, as well as his excellence on the field. Before 1999, it was called simply the NFL Man of the Year Award but after the death of superstar Walter Payton (having been the 1977 recipient himself), the award was renamed to honor his legacy as a humanitarian.

Each year, a winner is selected from one nominee from each of the 32 different teams. A panel of judges that includes the NFL, Walter Payton's widow, the winner from the year before, and a number of former players select the winner, who receives a $50,000 donation in his name to a charity of his choice.

Not many Americans are historians and very few know the details of America's amazing journey from the rebellion of 1776 to the volatile political scenario of the present, but everyone knows who Abraham Lincoln is and most understand his legacy. While an extremely intelligent man, his legacy is not based on policies but on his unwavering fortitude during the greatest crisis in American history. And while Payton was an outstanding football player, what he is remembered most for is being a humanitarian who helped make our society better.

YOUR SUCCESS IS DETERMINED BY YOUR FAILURES

Most experts and people believe that Abraham Lincoln was our greatest president ever, but not everyone is aware of his road to the White House and his many failures:

1816: His family was forced out of their home. He had to work to support them.

1818: His mother died.

1831: Failed in business.

1832: Ran for state legislature and lost. He also lost his job and wanted to go to law school but couldn't get in.

1833: Borrowed some money from a friend to begin a business and by the end of the year he was bankrupt. He spent the next 17 years of his life paying off this debt.

1834: Ran for state legislature again and won.

1835: Was engaged to be married, but his fiancée died.

1836: Had a total nervous breakdown and was in bed for six months.

1838: Tried to become speaker of the state legislature but lost.

1840: Sought to become an elector but lost.

1843: Ran for Congress and lost.

1846: Ran for Congress again and won.

1848: Ran for re-election to Congress and lost.

1849 Sought the job of land officer in his home state and lost.

1854: Ran for United States Senate and lost.

1856: Sought the Vice-Presidential nomination at the Republican national convention and got less than 100 votes.

1858: Ran for U.S. Senate again and lost again.

1860: Elected president of the United States.

Abraham Lincoln, our greatest president, was a world class failure. If Donald Trump had been around at the time, he probably would have called Lincoln a loser, but failure is often the key ingredient in success. His difficult road prepared him for the one thing he was destined to do: preserve our union. The most momentous event in U.S. history, the Civil War, started a month after Lincoln became president and ended a month after his assassination, meaning that the war raged on for 98% of his presidency. Even so, But he kept the country intact despite the best efforts of nearly everybody else to split it into pieces. No matter the pressure, no matter how bleak things looked, he never succumbed and he never wavered from his rock solid objective. Our nation is splintering now over things great and small and our president is exacerbating its collapse, but if we remember the lessons of Lincoln, we can preserve the union.

FAUSTIAN BARGAIN

Before Republicans and Democrats can approach each other to resolve issues as they are supposed to do, it is critical that Republicans stand up to Trump. After six months of Republican passivity during the beginning of the Trump Administration, principled conservatives started speaking up. Jeff Flake, a Republican senator from Arizona, who announced in October 2017 that he would be retiring, wrote the following insightful words in his book, *Conscience of a Conservative: A Reflection of Destructive Politics and A Return to Principle.*

> *"It was we conservatives who rightly and robustly asserted our constitutional prerogatives as a co-equal branch of government when a Democrat was in the White House but who, despite solemn vows to do the same in the event of a Trump presidency, have maintained an unnerving silence as instability has ensued. To carry on in the spring of 2017 as if what was happening was anything approaching normalcy required a determined suspension of critical faculties and tremendous powers of denial."[1]*

Flake believes that his party engages in a binary analysis: if it's bad for Democrats, then it must be good for Republicans. Democrats undergo the same thinking as well, Flake points out, and it is equally wrong, unproductive and contrary to the best interests of the country as a whole. He admits that standing silent while Trump wreaks havoc is cowardly and that principled people can no longer sit quietly on the sidelines.

> *"If by 2017, the conservative bargain was to go along for the very bumpy ride because with Congressional hegemony and the*

White House we had the numbers to achieve some long-held policy goals — even as we put at risk our institutions and our values — then it was a very real question whether any such policy victories wouldn't be Pyrrhic ones. If this was our Faustian bargain, then it was not worth it. If, ultimately, our principles were so malleable as to no longer be principles, then what was the point of political victories in the first place?" [2]

Flake was not the only Republican speaking up against Trump. In July of 2017, others started to do so as well. After months of controversies and record low approval ratings, it seemed that Trump's public humiliation of his own attorney general, Jeff Sessions, pushed some Republicans in Congress over some kind of line in the sand. Republican senators rushed to the cameras to defend not only Sessions' recusal as "the right thing" but his work as attorney general. At the same time that Congress passed a veto-proof sanctions law against Russia that tied Trump's hands on future actions with Russia, Congress also began to anticipate what Trump might do to slow down or shut down the Russia investigation. Slowly but surely, lawmakers and the president appeared to be going their separate ways, with some senators talking as though Trump had become almost irrelevant.

Then, of course, there was Charlottesville in August 2017 where Republican lawmakers came out of the woodwork to criticize the president. Many are beginning to realize that embracing chaos, instead of teamwork, will make governing much harder. Will it be enough to force the parties to work together? As Trump frequently says, *"Time will tell."*

In a September 1, 2017 op-ed in the *Washington Post*, Republican Senator John McCain wrote these insightful words:

"Our shared values define us more than our differences and acknowledging those shared values can see us through our challenges today if we have the wisdom to trust in them again...

We [Congress] seem convinced that majorities exist to impose their will with few concessions and that minorities exist to prevent the party in power from doing anything important. That's not how we were meant to govern. Our entire system of government... was designed for compromise... We can fight like hell for our ideas to prevail, but we have to respect each other or at least respect the fact that we need each other." [3]

The Republican maverick then made the following comments.

"That has never been truer than today, when Congress must govern with a president who has no experience of public office, is often poorly informed, and can be impulsive in his speech and conduct. We must respect his authority and constitutional responsibilities. We must, where we can, cooperate with him, but we are not his subordinates. We don't answer to him. We answer to the American people. We must be diligent in discharging our responsibility to serve as a check on his power, and we should value our identities as members of Congress more than our partisan affiliation." [4]

Despite these periodic criticisms, Republicans have chosen, for the most part, to remain silent even when the president is saying that we should only bring into the country people from countries like Norway instead of "shithole" countries like Africa or Haiti. Former Republican Congressman Joe Scarborough, host of the *Morning Joe* talk show, wrote in the *Washington Post* the next day: *"there can be no compromise or middle ground between those who defend the Constitution and a president who understands so little of what has made our nation great. The fight for America's future has begun and the time for rationalizing Trump's aberrant behavior is long past."* [5]

Rationalizing. Enabling. Complicit. Take your pick.

GEORGE'S OLD FRIEND

Lincoln was not only a great president and politician, he was a loving father and husband and a good friend. Sometimes politics separates families and friends but we must always remember our priorities. There are people I went to high school with who think differently than I do politically today. If I met them today, we might not be friends, but since I was a friend as a child, no matter what happens throughout my life, I will remain a friend forever.

The sad thing about the civil war was that families and friends were placed on opposite sides and into enemy camps. Many of the soldiers, and their leaders, had friends on the other side. Abraham Lincoln had been a friend with a Confederate General named George Pickett, who was instrumental at Gettysburg in 1863. Charles W. Moores tells the story, recounted in William Bennett's book *The Moral Compass*, of Lincoln visiting Pickett's home in Virginia while the war was still going on. His wife answered the door with a baby in her arms. Lincoln asked if this was George Pickett's home to which she replied, "Yes, and I am his wife and this is his baby."

"I am Abraham Lincoln," the president replied.

"The president!" Mrs. Pickett gasped.

"No," Lincoln replied. "Abraham Lincoln, George's old friend."

Lincoln held the baby for a few minutes as Mrs. Pickett stared in astonishment at the site. Finally, he gave the baby back to its mother and said to the child, "*Tell your father, the rascal, that I forgave him for the sake of your bright eyes.*"[6]

George Pickett was responsible for the deaths of hundreds of Union soldiers, but he had long been Lincoln's friend. Before we became Democrats and Republicans and engaged in political warfare with our "enemies," we were brothers and sisters, aunts and uncles, friends and colleagues. Is that still possible today?

CULTURAL CONFRONTATION

Amidst the never-ending chaos in the White House, in late July of 2017, Trump decided to double down on the premise that cultural issues could trump economic self-interest for blue-collar white voters that helped elect him. He continued to embrace the failed Senate effort to repeal the *Affordable Care Act*, despite abundant evidence that the most devoted of his base would be among the biggest losers in all of the Republican replacement plans. One day before the final attempt to repeal Obamacare, the Administration rolled back transgender and gay rights. Then, just a few hours after the vote, Trump engaged in a blistering attack on undocumented immigrant gang members, repeatedly calling them "animals" while calling for an unshackling of law enforcement from "pathetic" big city mayors.

Ironically, the failed effort to repeal Obamacare illustrated the dilemma the Republican party finds itself in. As a candidate, Trump promised to block cuts to Social Security, Medicare and Medicaid, but as president, he quickly deferred to congressional healthcare plans that hit hard at both blue-collar whites and older working adults, most of whom vote Republican.

By the same token, the expansion of Medicaid under Obamacare that brought in millions of low-income working adults made Medicaid critical to communities where Republicans dominate. Yet all of the GOP efforts to repeal Obamacare, with the exception of the Senate's final "skinny" repeal, not only rolled back Medicaid expansion but also imposed deep cuts. Even though they lost the battle on healthcare, Republicans may have dodged a bullet, because they would have had a hard time explaining to millions of their constituents why they lost their coverage and why their premiums were higher.

It appears, however, that Trump will continue to pursue cultural confrontation. In August 2017, Trump announced plans to crack down on Latino gang activity, urged police not to be "too nice'" in making arrests and the Justice Department's plan to pursue universities that have affirmative action policies it deems discriminatory to whites surfaced. On August 3, the White House revealed its plan to reduce the number of people who can immigrate to the country legally. Just as Hurricane Harvey was hitting landfall, the president pardoned former Sheriff Joe Arpaio, who would became a candidate for Senate in 2018, still claiming that Obama was born in Kenya. There were many other instances as well.

Occasionally, throwing red meat to his base allows Trump to remain insulated from conservative backlash. His approval rating in August 2017 among conservative Republicans nationally was almost exactly what it was on Inauguration Day, but aggressive appeals to cultural anxiety is risky and is not the answer. It is, in fact, a cynical and short-sighted distraction designed only to create a wedge between different segments of American society. America needs healing, not further division.

THE WORLD WILL NEVER FORGET

In December of 1862, one month before signing the Emancipation Proclamation, with the public turning against him and the war effort not going so well, Abraham Lincoln wrote Congress that the country faced two inseparable moral and political obligations. The first was to preserve the Union and the second was to free the slaves.

Repeating what he had said in his inaugural address, Lincoln wrote:

> *"One section of our country believes slavery is right and ought to be extended while the other believes it is wrong and ought not*

to be extended. This is the only substantial dispute… Physically speaking, we cannot separate. We cannot remove our respective sections from each other nor build an impassable wall between them." [7]

The same applies today. Democrats and Republicans cannot physically separate and it's not possible for them to divorce each other. He also acknowledged that the two sides could not continue to fight forever and that, to save the country, they had to figure out how to work together. Lincoln pointed out that his generation could not escape history and neither can ours.

"Fellow citizens, we cannot escape history. We of this Congress and this administration will be remembered in spite of ourselves. No personal significance, or insignificance, can spare one or another of us. The fiery trial through which we pass will light us down, in honor or dishonor, to the latest generation. We say we are for the Union. The world will not forget that we say this. We know how to save the Union… We shall nobly save, or meanly lose, the last best hope of earth." [8]

Today, we are not engaged in a great civil war but we have been divided more so than any time in our lifetimes. We know what we have to do, but no one wants to take the first step. It is easier to sling arrows at the other side than to come up with common-sense solutions.

On April 9, 1865, Confederate leader General Robert E. Lee and General Ulysses S. Grant, Commander of the Union Army, met at Appomattox Court House. The Union general granted Lee favorable terms of surrender, allowing the men to return to their homes and letting the officers, cavalrymen, and artillerymen keep their swords and horses if the men agreed to lay down their arms and abide by federal law. Grant even supplied food to the rebels, who were desperately low on rations. Soldiers on both sides cheered and cried upon hearing the news.

The formal ceremony took place on April 12 under the supervision of General Joshua Chamberlain. As the Confederate soldiers came forward to hand over their weapons, Chamberlain ordered his men to salute their defeated adversaries as a gesture of respect. After four years of pain, heartache, and blood, Lincoln allowed his former enemies to go home and the Union army saluted them in the process. It would be hard to imagine Democrats and Republicans, Christians and Muslims, or white supremacists and Black Lives Matter activists saluting each other. We are a divided society. Our divisions are partisan, religious, racial, ethnic, class-based, generational, and geographic, but like Lincoln, we must ensure that the union is preserved.

16

CONCLUSION (POST-GAME COMMENTARY)

"Government of the people, by the people, and for the people, shall not perish from the earth."
Abraham Lincoln

"Humanly speaking, it is impossible. But not with God. Everything is possible with God."
Jesus, Mark 10:27

"Take a nap every afternoon."
All I Really Need to Know I Learned in Kindergarten

Before a preseason game in 2016, San Francisco 49ers quarterback Colin Kaepernick sat down during the playing of the national anthem. During a post-game interview, he explained his position stating, "*I am not going to stand up to show pride in a flag for a country that oppresses black people and people of color. To me, this is bigger than football and it would be selfish on my part to look the other way."*

Since he was protesting the actions of local police departments and the criminal justice systems of states, his protest against the national government made no sense, especially since the government was, at the time, headed by a black president with a black attorney general. Nonetheless, Kaepernick continued this protest (although later kneeling instead of sitting) throughout the season and quickly became a polarizing figure. An NFL fan poll showed that Kaepernick was the most disliked player in the NFL and despite his indisputable athletic ability, when the 2017-2018 season started, no team had picked him up and Kaepernick became unemployed, unsure if he would ever play again.

On September 17, 2017, only four players, out of 1696, protested, but a political rally in Alabama on September 22 changed everything when President Trump gleefully called the protesters "sons of bitches." Over the next five days, the president doubled and tripled down and tweeted nearly two dozen times about "those" football players disrespecting "our" heritage.

As a veteran, I was totally against the way Kaepernick chose to protest, but I was much more disturbed by yet another action by the president to further divide us than I was by the protesters themselves. Two days after his comments, hundreds of players, both black and white, as well as coaches and owners, knelt, locked arms and pledged unity. Superstar Tom Brady, a friend of Trump's, said that the president's comments were "divisive." In the aftermath of Charlottesville, the president said that there were "good people" on "both sides," which begs the question: were some of the NFL protesters "good people" or were they all "sons of bitches?"

For weeks, America was again divided. Sadly, divisiveness works in politics. However, it solves nothing, accomplishes nothing, and leaves only a wake of destruction in its path. Like the NFL, there is much polarization in the United States along racial, ethnic, economic, partisan, and other lines. While nobody wants to take any blame for the nation's ills, everyone is all too eager to assign blame. This book has tried to figure out why we are so divided and has attempted to find solutions. I certainly don't have all the answers, but it is obvious that our country is splintered and fractured. We will not remain a great country if we pit one segment of society against another. We must always seek the truth and ask ourselves if our kids, Jesus and Abraham Lincoln would approve of our decisions. If the answer is yes, we're on the right track.

THE GREATEST COUNTRY IN HISTORY

In almost every measurable way, the United States is the greatest country in the history of the world, although its record is certainly not spotless. Our European ancestors exploited Native Americans and ran them off their land. From Colonial times to Appomattox, our government permitted certain citizens to own other human beings as property. At its ratification in 1789, our amazing Constitution specifically allowed the importation of slaves to continue, and in fact, made this particular section of the Constitution the only section not subject to modification. And shamefully, our Founding Fathers decreed that the value of Negro slaves was 3/5 of the white population, a fact despicable in its own right, but one that also gave slave states more representation in Congress and more influence in the Electoral College.

Despite certain deficiencies, however, the United States is the most democratic and idealistic nation that has ever existed, as well as being the richest and most powerful country the world has ever seen. From its founding, where 13 separate states embarked upon an experiment to unite together, to the Civil War, where 600,000 young men died over whether the country would stay united or dissolve, to World War II, when the nation was threatened by fascism, to September 11, 2001, the United States has always been a beacon of freedom for all the world.

However, we have always been, in many ways, a nation divided and there have always been competing theories and voices about the issues of the day. From the battles between Alexander Hamilton and Thomas Jefferson over the strength of the federal government, to the debates between Abraham Lincoln and Steven Douglas over the future of slavery, to the New Deal of FDR and the counterrevolution of Ronald Reagan concerning the role of government, to the 2000 election between George W. Bush and Al Gore, decided by one Supreme Court Justice, to the volatile 2016 presidential election, we have always been a fractured society.

American history has always moved in cycles, fluctuating from periods of conservatism or "normalcy" to times of liberalism or "activism." There have always been battles between the rights of the many versus the rights of the few, between rich and poor, Democrats versus Republicans. What has made the last 40 years different is the cultural war that has divided our nation into red states and blue states. Many no longer debate the issues as "right" or "wrong," but characterize the people involved as "good" and "bad."

I have looked to our nation's leaders in recent years for solutions to complex problems and have grown increasingly dismayed at what I have seen. Instead of offering solutions and leadership, our country's politicians point their fingers at each other, blaming the other side for messes that they themselves accept no responsibility for. Instead of trying to persuade us that their adversary's policies are misguided, they instead try to convince us that their opponent is evil. While mud-slinging works in the short term, in the long run it only creates distrust and cynicism and no one benefits. The ultimate result of all this mud-slinging is Donald Trump.

We are a nation of over 300 million, ethnically and religiously diverse as the sands on the beach and, in the age of the Internet, an incredibly fragmented society. We are southerners and northerners, doctors, farmers and mechanics, white and black, rich and poor, Christian and Jewish, young and old, educated and uneducated. There are a thousand other things that separate us. The solution, in the governmental context, is to find what binds us together, focusing on what we have in common. As a Christian, I eagerly await the day when Jesus will rule and reign. Until then, it's up to us and while human government will always come up short, it is inexcusable to do nothing. We must try to solve our problems, if not for our sake, for our children's sake.

While you and I may lean towards one policy or philosophy as opposed to another, we must remember that we are on the same team and work towards common goals. We cannot sit back and claim that the government is misguided, crooked, wrong, etc. and do nothing ourselves. We cannot let Trump embarrass and harm this country week after week and do and say nothing. In the New Testament book of James, the author writes that if we know what is right but do nothing, our omissions are just as wrong as our acts of commission. In the same way, if we know that our president is acting improperly, and we do nothing, our omissions, and especially the omissions of those in Congress, are wrong. We must speak up, we must be heard and our words must be guided not by party but by country, not by partisanship but by patriotism.

Most Americans want a better future for their children. Most Americans love their country and want it to be a beacon to the world. Most Americans believe in one God. We have one future, one nation, one God. Asked to explain the difference between a civilized society and a barbaric one, Aristotle said that a barbaric culture lives from day-to-day, consuming what it plunders. However, But in a civilized society, people plan and work for the next generation, hoping to create a better world for their children. Are we civilized or barbaric? The answer is not clear.

The differences between the two sides stem from deeply held opinions about what makes good people and a good nation. The issue is the very notion of what morality is and how it applies to the government. There is one thing that everyone can agree on: raising our children to be responsible, compassionate adults.

Over 150 years ago, Alexis de Tocqueville, trying to figure out what made America great, made the following observations:

"I sought for the key to the greatness and genius of America in her harbors... in her fertile fields... in her rich mines and vast world commerce; in her public-school system and institutions of learning. I sought for it in her democratic Congress and in her matchless institutions. Not until I went into the churches of America and heard her pulpits sing with righteousness did I understand the secret of her genius and power. America is great because America is good, and if America ever ceases to be good, America will cease to be great." [1]

To be a great nation, we must unite Americans around common hopes instead of dividing them by their economic and cultural fears. America is great and has been since 1776. The tougher question: is America good?

STRAIGHTENING THE SHIP

Partisanship will never completely go away and our nation will most likely never be totally indivisible, but if we are determined to create a "more perfect union," if we are willing to focus on God and country as the foundation and pursue responsibility and compassion as a team, it can be done. If we ask ourselves, *"Is it right?"* it can be done. If we realize that "people like me" includes all of us, it can be done. If we really understand and accept the meaning of *e pluribus unum*, it can be done. If we become Good Samaritans like Mattress Mack, it can be done. If we become the Nathans of today to challenge our leaders when necessary, it can be done. If we're willing to tell the truth when the Emperor is wearing no clothes, it can be done. If we realize that all people have a right to healthcare, that climate change is not a hoax and that diplomacy is just as important as a strong military, it can be done. If we recognize the importance of work, acknowledge that poverty affects us all, and that saddling the next generation with debilitating debt is immoral, it can be done. If we're willing to insist on the truth and pursue policies that Jesus, our kids and Lincoln would approve of, it can be done. If we will ask *"Where does it hurt?"* it can be done.

However, if we're not willing to work towards a 100% America, or if we don't care about the world we leave to the next generation, if we insist on squandering the world's resources, or if we accept living in a post-truth world, if we are not willing to be our brother's keeper, if we continuously say it's not my problem, if we try to live in a bubble outside of the world community and divide everyone into groups of "winners" and "losers," if we try to blame all of our problems on "those people" from "shithole" countries, if we allow our president to lie and assault our institutions, it cannot be done.

While you and I may lean towards one policy or philosophy as opposed to another, we must remember that we are on the same team. For the sake of our children, we must create a healthcare system that works for every single American. So that future Americans are not terrorized by would-be Osama bin Ladens or crazy dictators like Kim Jong-Un, we must have a foreign policy that is strong and just, rather than strong and arrogant. If we are to bequeath an America that is the most powerful country in the world, we must insure that our energy policies are based in the future rather than the past. If we intend to leave behind the natural beauty of the world that God created for us, we must pursue sound environmental policies. If we are to grow the economy and provide as many Americans as possible with jobs that provide dignity, we must rebuild our infrastructure and focus on renewable energy. If we want to claim that we are a moral nation, then we must provide a safety net for the poor and reduce the deficits and debt.

Many people blame our leaders and say the fault lies with the White House or the Congress. They would be correct, especially during the era of Trump, but some of the biggest reasons for the faults of our government do not lie with our leaders but with ourselves. If you want to understand at least part of the problem, look in the mirror.

SOCIAL CONTRACT

John Locke said that government is a social contract and under this theory, the consent of the governed is the only true basis of any sovereign's right to rule. Locke said that people form governments to preserve life, liberty and property and to insure justice. If the government acts improperly, it breaks the contract with the people and no longer enjoys their consent. Locke's ideas are even more valid today than when he wrote them in the late 17th century.

For the first 150 or so years of this nation, the federal government had few responsibilities and the people expected little of it beyond national defense, printing money and collecting tariffs. In 1790, its population was just under four million. In 1860, it was 31 million. By 1945, the population had grown to 140 million, to 227 million by 1980 and to 323 million by 2016. Now, life is far more complicated than it used to be.

When Teddy Roosevelt took office, the federal government was spending just over $500 million a year and people looked mostly to state and local government to deal with social and economic issues.[2] The progressive movement that sprung up in the early 1900s took on a host of issues, including anti-trust actions, labor laws to protect women and children, prohibition, and the 17th amendment that allowed citizens to vote directly for U.S. Senators. The 16th amendment authorized an income tax and, although it was quite modest by today's standards, it provided a constitutional means of financing the growth of the government. A generation later, the government had no choice but to grow in response to the Great Depression. Through Roosevelt's New Deal, dozens of government programs sprung up overnight. Since FDR, Americans have looked to the government for solutions to all of their problems. Although Reagan proclaimed that government was the problem rather than the solution, government continued to grow even during his tenure. In the aftermath of the failure to repeal Obamacare, "Medicare for All" may further cause the public to rely upon the government.

Government cannot cure all ills, especially since we have many conflicting and opposing viewpoints and since we are going further and further into debt. In the not-too-distant future, whites will become the minority. Dozens of languages are spoken in our schools and the gap between rich and poor continues to grow wider. There are many divisions in our society and we are not united. In order to bridge these gaps, we need leadership not just from politicians, but from you and I as well. But people are hard to please. They want less government but they don't want less Social Security. They want lower taxes and yet better roads. They want better education for their children, but lower school expenditures. They want to reduce the debt but want free healthcare and pay lower taxes. It's a tricky task getting everything in balance.

History shows us that crises change things. For example, the Civil War led to the dismantling of the slavery system and to the passage of the 13th, 14th, and 15th Amendments, which eliminated slavery, created the concept of equal protection for all and gave the right to vote to former slaves, respectively. The Great Depression led to the New Deal and a much more active government. The Watergate scandal resulted in stricter ethics laws that led to the removal of many elected officials. September 11th has affected every aspect of our society in ways that have still not manifested themselves. In the years to come, we will have to deal with the legacy of debt we're leaving our children and the growing poverty rate. Lastly, we'll have to deal with the inevitable consequences of the post-truth, *America First* Trump presidency that has divided the country into two tribes.

The U.S. is like a huge corporation and every one of us is a shareholder. We don't have time to deal with "the business" and so we let a board of directors (Congress) make decisions for us. While they may not intentionally desire to harm us, they often do, because we're silent about our needs and desires. Whose fault is that? Our leaders? Or does the blame lie with us for not getting involved? The answer is both. Although you'll rarely hear a candidate say that the problem is you, a president does not lie to a nation in a vacuum; the country must allow it to happen, but as luck would have it, you're also part of the solution.

Our entire system of government is based upon three simple words that will stand the test of time: *"We, the people."* Not some of the people, not just the rich people, and not just the powerful people, but all of us. When Jefferson wrote that governments derive their just powers from the consent of the governed, he was talking about you and I.

I believe Donald Trump is a serial liar who has wreaked havoc on this nation. While there may be legal justification for his term to end prematurely, I have a crazy suggestion until that day. Let's pray for him and all of our leaders that they will be truthful and govern in a way that will honor God and take into account every single American. No matter who is in office, whether they are of our political party or not, the Bible commands us to respect and honor them. Romans 13:1 says, *"Everyone must submit to governing authorities. For all authority comes from God and those in positions of authority have been placed there by God."*

Since I have blasted Trump in no uncertain terms, there could be accusations of hypocrisy on my part, but I hope he succeeds and I frequently pray for him. Since he is the pilot of the American plane, so to speak, it benefits no one, including me, if the plane crashes. While I hope he succeeds and changes course, I don't see any sign of that happening. In fact, many candidates running in 2018 are going out of their way to emulate or even out-Trump Trump. "Drain the swamp," "build the wall," many candidates are shouting. "Rigged system," "fake news," "America first," they're loudly proclaiming. In a desperate bid for "authenticity," candidates are cursing, insulting and threatening while previously admired demonstrations of restraint and polish are considered weakness. According to Russ Schreifer, an adviser to Mitt Romney and George W. Bush, "Now, it's less about who's more conservative and more about who's going to adhere to the Trump agenda and the Trump ideology. Candidates now seem most comfortable talking about vanquishing their enemies than they do about governing."[3] And even though she hasn't had a job in five years, many GOP candidates are focusing their campaigns on Hillary Clinton. "We don't need to investigate our president. We need to arrest Hillary," claims an ad for Don Blankenship, West Virginia senate candidate.[4]

Hillary Clinton was an extremely flawed candidate, but shouting "lock her up" in 2018 is not the answer to this country's many problems. Labeling Americans who think differently as enemies is not the solution and "vanquishing" them will not make us stronger. We're better than that. We have real and complex problems. As a concerned citizen, I am speaking up, and will continue to speak up. I hope you will, too, regardless of party. Ignoring, condoning and imitating bad conduct does not make us patriots and winners; it makes us cowards and losers.

COMEBACK

In the 2017 Super Bowl, one of the greatest teams in NFL history, the New England Patriots, was behind 28-3 in the third quarter. Their all-star quarterback, Tom Brady, had a poor first half. I remember yelling at my TV set in the third period as the Patriots were methodically running the ball and throwing short passes. I thought this was the wrong strategy since they were so far behind. They had to throw long passes, I thought, and try to get back in the game. Time was against them, but unflappable Brady kept doing what he does and the team kept doing what they had practiced so many thousands of times. Yard by yard, point by point, minute by minute, they kept plugging away, doing what they had been trained to do. Eventually when the clock ran out, they had tied the game and the Super Bowl had its first overtime game in its history. The Patriots won the toss and scored on its first drive for their fifth Super Bowl victory.

We can come back as a nation as well, but we first have to admit to ourselves that partisan bickering and non-stop attacks aren't working. We have to look in the mirror and realize that part of the problem lies within. There's a branch of science known as cartoon thermodynamics, discovered by the late film critic Roger Ebert, which states: *"Any body suspended in space will remain in space until made aware of its situation."* In other words, Wile E. Coyote can fall off a cliff and hover in midair until he looks down, at which point he will start to plummet. That is where our political system is now or will soon be. Congress as a whole has not yet looked down and come face to face with the reality of political gravity and truly appreciate just how chaotic and wackadoodle Donald Trump has made everything. Until this happens, and unless changes are made, even the Road Runner won't be able to help.

Former Republican Congressman and current host of *Morning Joe*, Joe Scarborough, wrote the following in the *Washington Post* on January 5, 2018:

> *"The world wonders how the United States will survive Donald Trump. And I ask, what will finally move Republicans to deliver a non-negotiable ultimatum to this unstable president? Will they dare place their country's interests above their own political fears? Or will they move to end this American tragedy only when there is nothing left to lose?"* [5]

"What will it take?" is an excellent question to ask of Republican leaders. Will they place the country's interests ahead of theirs? It doesn't seem hopeful. Trump himself seems virtually incapable of self-corrections or making any adjustments and constantly complains that he doesn't get proper credit for accomplishments. But he's not criticized because the stock market is up or because ISIS has been defeated in Iraq; he is criticized because he either tries to take complete credit when he only deserves partial credit or because he insults and attacks everybody.

Trump has ripped this nation apart along cultural and racial lines and apparently has concluded that this is governing. Such a strategy no doubt alienated anyone who was not already in his corner and will not win him new supporters. Not only has he been unable to reach out beyond his own core base, he hasn't even tried. Whatever good press his substantive policies are entitled to are unfortunately overwhelmed and drowned out by the constant whirlwind of score-settling, divisive rhetoric, and finger-pointing. Trump's approval ratings have consistently been the lowest of any elected president's but not because of an unfair, fake media. His achievements are simply outweighed, and will continue to be outweighed, by the deeply set views that his 24/7 reality show has caused millions of Americans to hold against him. If he and his staff continue instead to lash out at a constant stream of enemies, his presidency will remain chaotic and unproductive. Unfortunately, all of America will suffer.

We need a government that inspires us, tells the truth, gets rid of all that is fake and does away with darkness. We need a government that unites rather than divides and looks to our friends for help. We need policies that will benefit the most Americans, that are steeped in truth, that Lincoln and Jesus would support, that will benefit our kids and grandkids. We need policies where healthcare is a right for all rather than a privilege for a few, where foreign relations are based on moral foundations as well as military might, where our government accepts, along with the rest of the world, the fact that human activity is contributing to climate change, where we put our people to work in jobs of the future and not the past, and where we are prudent and responsible with our budgets but compassionate with the neediest members of our society.

SOLID FOUNDATION: TRUTH AND TRUST

Our country is approaching a critical time in its history. I've consistently bashed Trump in this book but do not support impeachment by Democrats only, which will only make our toxic political system worse. Unfortunately, it appears that most Republicans are inclined to look the other way because they're getting certain things that they want from Trump, such as tax cuts, Supreme Court Justices, etc. Christians who support Trump's policies but are troubled by his words justify it by stressing the importance of extending grace to Trump. German theologian Dietrich Bonhoeffer, however, would have called it "cheap grace." On this side of heaven, there is a flip side to grace and forgiveness: repentance, contrition and accountability, for without those it's nothing more than closing one's eyes. French novelist Paul Bourget once said that "*One must live the way one thinks or end up thinking the way one has lived.*" If you allow outrageousness, divisiveness, lies and hatred to continue unabated, you've made a choice on how you and your children will live.

The foundation of our country is cracked and it must be rebuilt on truth and trust. The solution lies with principled Republicans. But if they don't step up in 2018, things will only get worse and the destructiveness of our broken system will accelerate.

Ohio Governor John Kasich has pointed out that, "*We can't pick and choose among half-truths and utter falsehoods and grab only the ones that reinforce our preconceived notions or stoke our shared fears. We can't live in our own reality.*" The truth, he added, is absolute and "*there is no path forward unless we are guided by the truth.*"[6]

During the debate in 2017 about repealing Obamacare, Senator John McCain made a speech for the parties to work together and trust one another.

"Let's trust each other. Let's return to regular order. We've been spinning our wheels on too many important issues because we keep trying to find a way to win without help from across the aisle. That's an approach that's been employed by both sides, mandating legislation from the top down, without any support from the other side, with all the parliamentary maneuvers that requires. We're getting nothing done."[7]

In a stunning speech on the Senate floor on January 17, 2018, Senator Jeff Flake threw out this challenge.

"No longer can we compound attacks on truth with our silent acquiescence. No longer can we turn a blind eye or a deaf ear to these assaults on our institutions... Together, united in the purpose to do our jobs under the Constitution, without regard to party or party loyalty, let us resolve to be allies of the truth and not partners in its destruction."[8]

Scarborough, Kasich, McCain, Flake and a few others realize that without truth and trust, our foundation will collapse. In the Sermon on the Mount, Jesus compared those who listened to his teaching with a person who built a house on solid rock. When the rains come, it will stand firm and not collapse. But for those who do not listen, they are like a person who builds a house on sand. When the storms come, it will *"collapse with a mighty crash."* Without truth and trust, there is no foundation and our beautiful and incredible nation will one day collapse.

Colin Kaepernick was right that our nation has problems. His solution, however, solved nothing, unnecessarily divided people and was dead wrong. Donald Trump's non-stop attempts to divide us are wrong as well and we must speak up and say so regardless of party. We must insist on truth, reject zero-sum politics and combat the moral midgetry of tribalism. We've had enough of the government's perpetual food fight. We are not two tribes of winners and losers with a sick system dominated by a

Deep State that seeks isolation, buries science, and abdicates its role as global leader. We know that facts matter, that words defile, and that objective truth must control. We are all shareholders in USA, Inc., and we insist that CEO Trump and the Board (Congress) act in our best interests and keep us in the loop. If they don't, we're going to step up to the plate. Like Carson Wentz, we're going to support our teammates whether or not we get the credit. Like Lance Armstrong's teammates, we're going to speak up if someone is hurting the team. We're looking to the future and not the past. We're one nation, we have one God, and one future. We are indivisible. We're Team America, and we're going to the Super Bowl!

FOOTNOTES

Preface

1. *2016 Pew Research Center Poll on Partisanship and Political Animosity in 2016;* www.people-press.org

Chapter 1

1. Winston Churchill, *The Gathering Storm* (Houghton Mifflin Harcourt) (1986) page 16.

2. Martin Luther King, Quoted in *American Gospel*, Jon Meacham (Random House) (2006) page 179.

3. Jim Wallis, *God's Politics: Why the Right Gets It Wrong and the Left Doesn't Get It* (Harper San Francisco) (2005) page 326.

4. Arthur M. Schlesinger, Jr., *The Cycles of American History* (Houghton Mifflin) (1986) page 23.

5. John F. Kennedy, *Profiles In Courage* (Harper & Brothers) (1955).

6. Daily Stormer, August 14, 2017.

7. Washington Post, August 14, 2017.

8. The Hill, August 12, 2017.

9. CBS News, August 31, 2017.

10. Southern Poverty Law Center report, *The Trump Effect: The Impact of the 2016 Election On Our Nation's Schools* (2017).

11. Ibid.

12. New York Times, *"Trump Alarms Lawmakers With Disparaging Words for Haiti and Africa,"* January 11, 2018.

13. CNN, Kaitlan Collins, January 11, 2018.

14. Ronald Brownstein, The Atlantic, *"The Tragedy of President Trump's Tribalism,"* November 2, 2017.

15. Judge George Daniels, U.S. District Court, Southern District of New York, *Citizens for Responsibility and Ethics in Washington v. Trump,* December 21, 2017.

16. Andrew Sullivan, New York Magazine, *"America Wasn't Built For Humans,"* September 19, 2017.

17. John Danforth, Washington Post Op-Ed, August 25, 2017.

18. Ibid.

19. Senator Jeff Flake, Speech on Senate Floor, October 26, 2017.

20. Washington Post, Senator Jeff Flake, October 27, 2017.

21. Public Policy Polling, October 31, 2017.

22. New York Times, December 9, 2017.

23. Bloomberg, Quoting Senator Bob Corker, April 18, 2018.

24. James Comey, *A Higher Loyalty: Truth, Lies and Leadership* (Macmillan Publishing) (2018)

25. Senator Jeff Flake, Speech on Senate Floor, October 26, 2017.

26. Newsweek Magazine, Quoting Charles Dent, December 24, 2017.

27. Washington Post, Quoting Senator Bob Corker, March 21, 2018.

28. Wakefield Research, May 10, 2017.

29. Washington Examiner, Quoting John McCain, January 20, 2018.

30. The Hill, January 20, 2018.

31. USA Today, Quoting Senator John McCain, March 21, 2018.

32. New York Times, quoting John Brennan, March 19, 2018.

33. New York Times, quoting Gary Schmitt, March 19, 2018.

34. New York Times, quoting Richard Haass, March 23, 2018.

35. Axios, April 6, 2018.

36. Watergate Committee Report, June 27, 1973, Rep. Lawrence Hogan, reported in *The Hill*, March 15, 2018.

37. Travis Tygart, U.S. Anti-Doping Agency Report, October 10, 2012.

38. Carson Wentz tweet, February 4, 2018.

Chapter 2

1. *Sports Illustrated*, National Football League's Mild Traumatic Brain Injury Committee Report (1994)

2. *Neurosurgery*, Dr. Benet Omalu (2005)

3. National Football League Survey (2008)

4. National Football League, Jeff Pash (2013)

5. Oxford Dictionary 2016 word of the year.

6. CNN, interview with Senator Bob Corker, October 24, 2017.

7. Senator Jeff Flake, Speech on Senate Floor, January 2018.

8. New York Times, June 23, 2017.

9. Washington Post, January 19, 2018.

10. Washington Post, January 2, 2018.

11. James R. Arnold, *Moro War: How America Battled A Muslim Insurgency in the Philippine Jungle 1902-1913*.

12. GovTrack.com

13. Washington Post, August 10, 2017.

14. Politico, March 15, 2018.

15. Washington Post, January 2, 2018.

16. Johnny Enlow, May 2017.

Chapter 3

1. Gallup, Knight Foundation poll (January 2018)

2. Monmouth University Poll, April 2, 2018.

3. Senator Jeff Flake, Speech on Senate Floor, October 26, 2017.

4. Washington Post, John McCain, January 17, 2018.

5. Business Insider, Michael McFaul, August 6, 2017.

6. Roll Call, Rep. Claudia Tenney, March 22, 2018.

7. The Hill, Rep. Steve Scalise, March 20, 2018.

8. Monmouth University poll (March 2018)

9. Washington Post, August 10, 2017.

10. Lyceum Address, Abraham Lincoln, January 27, 1838

11. New York Post, Jerry Falwell, Jr., August 21, 2017.

12. ABC This Week, Jerry Falwell, Jr., August 20, 2017.

13. Faith and Freedom Coalition Conference, Ralph Reed, June 10, 2016.

14. The American Conservative, Rod Dreher.

15. Ibid.

16. Johnny Enlow, January 1, 2018.

17. The American Conservative, Rod Dreher.

18. *CNN,* Erin Burnett "Out-Front," Tony Perkins, March 20, 2018.

19. *CNN,* Peter Wehner, March 20, 2018.

Chapter 4

1. Henry Kissinger, *Diplomacy* (Simon & Schuster) 1994, page 17.

2. *Foreign Affairs*, Samuel R. Berger, May/June 2004, page 48.

3. Harry Truman, Quoted in *The Good Fight*, Peter Berger (Harper Collins) 2006, page 10.

4. *The Good Fight,* Peter Berger, page 10.

5. Ibid, page 12.

6. Council on Foreign Relations, April 11, 2017.

7. u-s-history.com, America First Committee.

8. The Guardian, January 18, 2018.

9. Richard Haass, Interview with Anderson Cooper (January 2018)

10. Wall Street Journal, Gary Cohn and H.R. McMaster (May 31, 2017)

11. CBS Evening News, Interview with John Kerry, June 1, 2017.

12. Harry Truman, Address to U.N., June 26, 1945.

13. Nikki Haley speech at U.N., December 21, 2017.

14. CNN, quoting Theresa May, November 30, 2017.

15. The Hill, Quoting David Duke, November 29, 2017.

Chapter 5

1. Elitedaily.com, January 2018.

2. The Daily Beast, December 28, 2017.

3. Washington Examiner, June 28, 2017.

4. Reuters, January 16, 2018.

5. CNN, March 14, 2018.

6. CNBC, March 21, 2018.

7. Ibid.

8. USA Today, September 6, 2017.

9. Barbara Perry, University of Virginia, April 5, 2017.

10. ProPublica, March 2018.

11. Tribune News Service, January 2, 2018.

12. NPR, November 17, 2017.

13. New York Times, interview with Walter Schaub, June 17, 2017.

14. Washington Post, December 19, 2017.

Chapter 6

1. *Restoring Fiscal Sanity*, Chapter Four ("Health"), Henry J. Aaron and Jack Meyer, page 74.

2. Ibid.

3. Ibid.

4. Washington Post, Joe Biden, July 17, 2017.

5. Senator John McCain, House Floor, July 25, 2017.

6. Ibid.

7. *Healthcare*, Janelle Bouie, October 17, 2017.

8. Kaiser Family Foundation, "*An Early Look at 2018 Premium Changes and Insurer Participation on ACA   Exchanges,*" August 10, 2017.

9. Washington Post, Joe Biden, July 17, 2017.

10. Pew Research Center, January 2017.

11. Washington Post, John Kasich and John Hickenlooper, June 20, 2017.

Chapter 7

1. *The Mighty and the Almighty: Reflections on America, God and World Affairs*, Madeline Albright with Bill Woodward (Harper Collins) 2006, Quoting Vaclev Havel, page 162.

2. Bloomberg Politics, "*At Trump's State Department, 8 of 10 Jobs Are Empty,*" March 13, 2018.

3. USA Today, "*…41 Countries That Don't Have A U.S. Ambassador,*" March 6, 2018.

4. Reuters, "*Defense Secretary Mattis Suggests Sticking With Iran Nuclear Deal,*" October 3, 2017.

5. New York Times, "*Why Decertifying The Iran Nuclear Deal Would Be A Bad Idea,*" October 5, 2017.

6. Fox News, Judith Miller, February 27, 2018.

7. NBC News, report on Center for American Progress's Moscow Project, March 22, 2018.

8. CNN, March 14, 2018.

9. Ibid.

10. Washington Post, February 18, 2018.

11. Senate Foreign Relations Committee Report, January 10, 2018.

Chapter 8

1. Paris Climate Agreement, 21st Conference of the Parties of the UNFCCC, December 12, 2015.

2. New York Times, June 1, 2017.

3. Forbes Magazine, Maggie McGrath, May 31, 2017.

4. New York Times, *Scientists Fear Trump Will Dismiss Blunt Climate Report,*" August 8, 2017.

5. National Climate Assessment (2017).

6. The Verge, *How Did Hurricane Harvey Get So Strong?*" August 25, 2017.

7. National Climate Assessment (2017).

8. Council On Foreign Relations, *The Consequences of Leaving the Paris Agreement,*" June 1, 2017.

9. National Intelligence Council, *Implications of U.S. National Security of Anticipated Climate Change,*" September 21, 2016.

10. Shiloh Fetzek, climateandsecurity.org.

11. U.S. Department of Defense Climate Change Adaptation Road Map (2014), reported in Vox, January 12, 2018.

12. Union of Concerned Scientists Report (2016), reported in Vox, January 12, 2018.

13. Foreign Policy Magazine, Anatol Lieven, January 2018.

14. Congressional Letter to the President, January 12, 2018.

15. "*Environment: Should We Go Green?*" www.publicagenda.com (2004), page 9.

16. "*Hurricanes and Climate Change,*" Union of Concerned Scientists, www.ususa.org/global_warming/science/hurricanes-and-climate-change.html (2005), page 3.

17. Ibid.

18. "*Global Warming,*" Union of Concerned Scientists, www.ususa.org/global_warming/science/global-warming-faq.html (2005), page 5.

19. Ibid, page 6.

20. Forbes Magazine, February 1, 2017.

21. *Plan B 2.0: Rescuing A Planet Under Stress and a Civilization in Trouble,* Lester R. Brown (W.W. Norton & Co.) 2006.

Chapter 9

1. Washington Post, Danielle Paquette, May 24, 2017.

2. New America, "*The Infrastructure Deficit,*" Samuel Sherraden, February 3, 2011.

3. Infrastructure Week 2017, Building America's Future, www.bafuture.org.

4. "*The 70 Year Trend in Federal Infrastructure,*" Eno Transportation Weekly, May 5, 2016.

5. Business Insider, "*Here's What The 'Pothole Tax' Costs The Average American Driver Every Year,*" Leanna Garfield, January 11, 2017.

6. Huffington Post, "*Investing In Infrastructure Can Create Jobs…*" May 17, 2017.

7. Environmental Defense Fund, "*Clean Energy Is Building A New America Workforce,*" www.edf.org (2015).

8. Ibid.

9. Ibid.

10. Ibid.

11. Department of Energy, U.S. Energy and Employment Report (2017)

12. Environmental Defense Fund, "*Clean Energy Is Building A New America Workforce*," www.edf.org (2015).

13. Ibid.

14. Inside Climate News, "*U.S. Renewable Energy Jobs Employ 800,000 People: In Charts*," Paul Horn, www.insideclimatenews.org.

15. Reuters, "*Exclusive: Trump's Coal Job Push Stumbles In Most States-Data*," January 19, 2018.

16. NRDC, "*U.S. Clean Energy Jobs Surpass Fossil Fuel Employment*," February 1, 2017.

17. Ibid.

18. Bloomberg Business, Brian Eckhouse and Tim Loh, November 8, 2017.

19. U.S. Energy Information Administration, Frequently Asked Questions, www.eia.gov.

20. California Senator Kevin de Leon, California Senate Floor, May 31, 2017.

Chapter 10

1. San Diego City Councilman Chris Ward, January 12, 2017.

2. CNN.com, March 16, 2018.

3. The Hill, Quoting Romina Boccia of the Heritage Foundation, March 23, 2018.

4. *Running on Empty: How the Democratic and Republican Parties Are Bankrupting Our Future and What Americans Can Do About It*, Peter J. Peterson (Farrar, Strauss and Giroux) 2004, page 43.

5. Ibid, page 49.

6. Ibid, page 62.

7. Fred.stlouis.org.

8. Reuters.com, "*U.S. Debt To Reach 150% of GDP in 30 Years-CBO*," May 30, 2017.

9. *Facing Up-How To Rescue the Economy From Crushing Debt & Restore The American Dream*, Peter Peterson (Simon & Schuster) 1993, page 114.

10. The Heritage Foundation, The 2013 Index of Dependence on Government, November 21, 2013.

11. United States Census (2014).

12. *American Mania: When More Is Not Enough*, Peter C. Wyman, M.D. (W.W. Norton Co.) 2005, Quoting the Children's Defense Fund Report, page 57.

13. Thoughtco.com, William Lloyd Garrison.

14. Committee for Responsible Federal Budget, October 2017.

15. Taxpolicycenter.org, "*Analysis of the Tax Cuts and Jobs Act.*"

16. Ibid.

17. Ibid.

18. Ibid.

19. Ibid.

20. Congressional Budget Office, reported in Vox, December 19, 2017.

21. Taxpolicycenter.org, "*Analysis of the Tax Cuts and Jobs Act.*"

22. Vox, December 19, 2017.

23. Ibid.

24. Concord Coalition, Statement from Director Robert Bixby, December 18, 2017.

25. Ibid.

26. Ibid.

27. Ibid.

Chapter 11

1. *Faith and Politics: How The Moral Values Debate Divides America And How To Move Forward Together*, John Danforth (Viking) 2006, page 154.

2. Ibid, page 165.

3. *Return To Greatness: How America Lost Its Sense of Purpose and What It Needs To Do To Recover It*, Alan Wolfe (Princeton University Press) 2005, page 165.

4. *The Two Americas: Our Current Political Deadlock and How To Break It*, Stanley B. Greenberg (Thomas Dunne Books) 2005, page 9.

5. *God's Politics: Why the Right Gets It Wrong and the Left Doesn't Get It,* Jim Wallis (Harper San Francisco) (2005) page 35.

6. Benjamin Franklin, Quoted in *America's God & Country, Encyclopedia of Quotations*, William J. Federer (Amerisearch, Inc.) 2000, page 250.

7. Benjamin Franklin, Quoted in *In God We Trust? Religion and American Political Life*, Edited by Corwin E. Smidt (Baker Academic) 2001, page 27.

8. Reinhold Niebuhr, Quoted in *Our Endangered Values: America's Moral Crisis*, Jimmy Carter (Simon & Schuster) 2005, page 59.

9. *Zorach v. Clauson*, 343 U.S. 306, 313 (1952), Quoted in *Divided By God: America's Church-State Problem And What We Should Do About It*, Noah Feldman (Farrar, Straus & Giroux) 2005, page 7.

10. Danforth, page 16.

11. Danforth, page 30-31.

12. CNN, John McCain, July 26, 2017.

13. New York Times, Quoting Michael Steele, September 11, 2017.

14. The Hill, January 24, 2018.

15. CNN Newsday, November 20, 2017.

16. Martin Luther King, quoted in *The Mighty and the Almighty: Reflections on America, God and World Affairs*, Madeline Albright with Bill Woodward (Harper Collins) 2006, page 47.

Chapter 12

1. California Civil Jury Instructions (CACI) 2017, Number 5003.

2. Washington Post, May 1, 2017.

3. Toronto Star, July 20, 2017.

4. New York Times, June 23, 2017.

5. New York Times, August 2, 2017.

6. Christian Ethics Today, *"What Lies Within: Post-Truth Evangelical Christianity,"* Bruce Gourley, February 2017.

7. Ibid.

8. Politico, January/February 2017.

9. AbrahamLincolnsclassroom.org.

Chapter 13

1. John Adams, Quoted in *In God We Trust? Religion and American Political Life*, Edited by Corwin E. Smidt (Baker Academic) 2001, page 49.

2. 36 U.S.C. Section 302 (1998).

3. *American Gospel*, Jon Meacham (Random House) 2006, page 15.

4. Ibid.

5. Ibid, page 5.

6. *Divided By God: America's Church-State Problem And What We Should Do About It,* Noah Feldman (Farrar, Straus & Giroux) 2005, page 237.

Chapter 14

1. "*The Conscience of the Nation Must Be Roused,*" Frederick Douglas, recounted in *The Book of Virtues: A Treasury of Great Moral Stories,* Edited by William J. Bennett (Simon & Schuster) 1993, pages 254-256.

Chapter 15

1. *Conscience of a Conservative: A Rejection of Destructive Politics and a Return to Principle,* Senator Jeff Flake (Random House) 2017.

2. Ibid.

3. Washington Post, Op-Ed, John McCain, September 1, 2017.

4. Ibid.

5. Washington Post, Op-Ed, Joe Scarborough, September 2, 2017.

6. "*George Pickett's Friend,*" Charles W. Moores, recounted in *The Moral Compass: Stories for a Life's Journey,* Edited by William J. Bennett (Simon & Schuster) 1995, page 656.

7. Abraham Lincoln, Annual Message to Congress, December 1, 1862.

8. Ibid.

Chapter 16

1. Alexis de Tocqueville, quoted in *America's God and Country, Encyclopedia of Quotations*, William J. Federer (Amerisearch, Inc.) 2000, page 204.

2. "*Events That Shaped The Century*," Our American Century (Time-Life Books) 1998, page 31.

3. New York Times, April 22, 2018.

4. Ibid.

5. Washington Post, Joe Scarborough, January 5, 2018.

6. *Two Paths: America Divided or United*, John Kasich (Thomas Dunne Books) 2017, page 11.

7. Senator John McCain, House Floor, July 25, 2017.

8. Senator Jeff Flake, Senate Floor, January 17, 2018.

ABOUT THE AUTHOR

Jim Hester has practiced law for more than 30 years; has taught law, business, and political science at six colleges and universities; has served on the boards of several charities and, as an army intelligence officer, served with the Green Berets and volunteered for the Persian Gulf War. He has worked, lived, and studied in numerous countries, has written both nonfiction and fiction books and, as the first person in his family to go to college, holds three graduate degrees.

Jim and his wife, Marla, live in San Diego and have four adult children. He is an avid student of history and of the Bible and is active in his church and community.

Jmhester13@gmail.com

CPSIA information can be obtained
at www.ICGtesting.com
Printed in the USA
BVHW051412051118
532196BV00015B/695/P

9 781628 655841